THE POSTNATAL EXERCISE BOOK

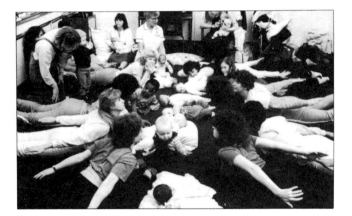

^{THE}POSTNATAL EXERCISE BOOK

A SIX MONTH FITNESS PROGRAM FOR NEW MOTHERS

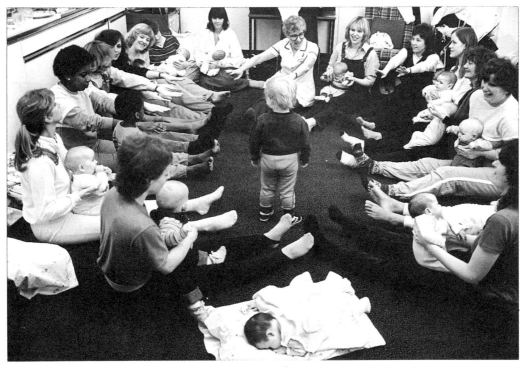

BARBARA WHITEFORD & MARGIE POLDEN

FOREWORD BY CAROLYN B. COULAM, M.D., THE MAYO CLINIC

PHOTOGRAPHS BY SANDRA LOUSADA

PANTHEON BOOKS, NEW YORK

Medical consultant Dr David Harvey

Text copyright © 1984 by Barbara Whiteford and Margie Polden
Photographs copyright © 1984 by Sandra Lousada
Illustrations copyright © 1984 by Frances Lincoln Limited
Foreword copyright © 1984 by Carolyn B. Coulam, M.D.
All rights reserved under International
and Pan-American Copyright Conventions

Published in the United States by Pantheon Books,
a division of Random House, Inc., New York

Originally published in Great Britain by
Century Publishing Co., London
Conceived, edited, and designed by Frances Lincoln Limited,
Apollo Works, 5 Charlton King's Road, London NW5 2SB, England

Library of Congress Cataloging in Publication Data
Whiteford, Barbara.
   The postnatal exercise book.
   Bibliography: p.
   Includes index.
   1. Postnatal care.   2. Exercise for women.
3. Physical fitness.   I. Polden, Margie.   II. Title.
RG801.W7   1984   646.7′5   84-42665

ISBN 0-394-72721-5

Manufactured in Italy
First American Edition

CONTENTS

Foreword by Carolyn B. Coulam, M.D.   6

Introduction   8

YOUR BODY BEFORE AND AFTER THE BIRTH   10

POSTURE AND BACK CARE   22

YOUR FEELINGS AFTER THE BIRTH   32

THE IMPORTANCE OF RELAXATION   38

GETTING STARTED
EXERCISES 0 TO 6 WEEKS   46
The first 48 hours – The post-Caesarean mother
At home – Daily exercise program
Your baby's physical needs

MAKING PROGRESS
EXERCISES 6 WEEKS TO 3 MONTHS   72
Lying on the floor – Sitting on the floor
On all fours – Standing up
Daily exercise program
Encouraging body control

FIT FOR LIFE
EXERCISES 3 TO 6 MONTHS   96
Pelvic floor control – Lying on the floor
Sitting on the floor – Kneeling exercises – The final test
At the swimming pool – Daily exercise program
Learning through play

Further reading   125

Useful addresses   125

Index   126

Acknowledgments   128

FOREWORD

The book you hold in your hands is the product of a revolution in obstetrics that began only twenty years ago. As late as the nineteenth century, postnatal exercise was thought to invite not only ill health but premature old age, and it was considered wrong to permit a recently delivered woman to return immediately to her customary level of activity. One or two days after giving birth, women were advised to rise from their beds and sit up for a period of time every day, according to their strength and inclination. This extremely mild activity was thought to be refreshing and to promote the natural discharges. But it was not considered prudent to indulge in walking until the womb and its ligaments had, to some degree, resumed their natural size and position. In any event, to walk before the fifth day was considered dangerous. According to conventional medical wisdom, lying in bed protected women from the "circulatory and nervous influences" (in the language of the day) that disordered the health. Few people paid much attention to the fact that women living in less industrialized nations made little or no change in their general conduct while pregnant and returned to their usual occupations almost immediately after delivery. The same had been true of women in ancient times, but that too was overlooked.

In the past, medical experts were concerned that exercise or activity immediately after delivery would weaken the pelvic structures. The idea of exercise to restore a woman's shape was almost unheard of, although as early as 1849 reference was made in an obstetrics textbook to the fact that an abdominal binder (or girdle) used immediately after delivery had no longterm effectiveness, while contracting the muscles did. As late as 1923, obstetrical texts encouraged bed rest for several days, and no mention was made of exercise to restore muscle tone.

It was not until 1962 that textbooks began to recommend exercises to restore the tone and strength of the abdominal muscles after pregnancy. Even then, a waiting period of six weeks was encouraged. Soon thereafter, postnatal exercises began to be advocated not only to restore the tone of the abdominal muscles but also to prevent pelvic prolapse and incontinence. Once thought to cause the relaxation of the pelvic floor, postnatal exercises have come full circle and are now prescribed correctly – for treatment of this same condition. In more recent texts, the recommended time span between delivery and exercise has become shorter and shorter, until a current obstetrical textbook states that exercises should preferably be started the day after delivery.

The Postnatal Exercise Book begins with gentle exercises that a woman can do in her hospital bed the day after her baby is born and goes on to offer increasingly challenging exercises for the next six months. In addition to taking physical changes into account, the authors show a unique sensitivity to the feelings and emotions of the postpartum woman and focus much more than other books on the relationship between mother and child. This new perspective makes *The Postnatal Exercise Book* a joy to use and an excellent addition to every new mother's library.

Carolyn B. Coulam, M.D.
Department of Obstetrics and
Gynecology
Mayo Clinic

INTRODUCTION

The drama of birth is the climax of nine long months of waiting and preparation for all mothers; you know that your life will never be quite the same. Lying there with your baby, you may feel new energy, relief and euphoria, or perhaps you just feel exhausted, homesick and sore. Whatever your feelings, you were probably prepared for them by your prenatal classes, or from books you read or the experience of friends. You will be expecting abnormal intensity of moods as an inevitable part of the emotional upheaval. However, you may have thought that after your baby was born, at least your body would return to normal right away. You remember yourself as you were before pregnancy – firm and upright. You watched with pride your blooming, expanding abdomen and breasts as pregnancy advanced, but now the birth is over you expected to find yourself back as you were. Instead you are faced with a third stage – flabby, slouching and droopy, a woman whom you barely recognize.

Although you may only just be beginning to realize how much has to be done for your small, utterly dependent baby, you also know that you will need to do something positive for yourself to return to the way you were. For nine months your body was adapting to carry the growing baby; fortunately it does not take nearly as long to restore it to normal. Some of the changes occur within hours of your baby's birth: the uterus starts contracting down immediately, returning to its normal size by about six weeks; you will also lose a large amount of fluid in the days immediately following delivery. Even so, your muscles will still look and feel slack, stretched and weak. How quickly these return to normal appearance and function will depend a little on nature, but mostly on you.

Using the exercises

The exercises in this book are carefully graded to suit you from immediately after the birth right up to six months later, when your body is strong again. Of course, you should check with a physician before beginning any exercise program, and if you are not used to exercising at all, get his or her advice as to your individual ability to move through the program, especially if you have had a previous history of back problems.

The subdivision into three sections (0-6 weeks, 6 weeks to 3 months, 3-6 months) only offers you a rough guide and is designed for the average woman and her rate of progress. If, for example, you are an older mother, or perhaps one who has had a Caesarean section, or if you took very little exercise prior to and during your pregnancy, then you will need to spend longer on the early exercises, perfecting them before moving on to the next stage. On the other hand, if you are a young mother who exercised regularly right up to a vaginal delivery, then you may feel able to advance to the second and then third stages a week or so earlier than suggested. Some useful ways of testing the strength of your important muscles are included to help you assess your own progress. Remember, too, that even if you did not feel like starting your exercises immediately, or even weeks after the birth, it is never too late to start.

Arranging your exercise schedule

If this is your first baby you may be surprised just how totally absorbing, and possibly frustrating, you find your new role. You cannot hear a baby's cry without assuming that it must be yours; you cannot go out for more than a few minutes for fear that you will be needed and you strongly believe that no one else can comfort your baby. All these feelings are normal and natural, and it follows that any program of exercises must not force you into unwanted and uncomfortable separation from your baby. All the exercises in this book are designed to be done at home, without the use of any equipment other than the usual household furniture.

Helping your baby's development

Alongside your own exercises, there are recommended positions, handling and play for your baby at the relevant stages of development. Just as in labor, when your knowledge enables you to direct your energy to coping with the contractions, if you are informed and confident in the handling of your baby, you will be more energetic, relaxed and fulfilled as a mother, and your baby will feel more secure and thus more contented in your care.

Rest and relaxation

Rest and relaxation are as vital as exercise in the early stages after birth, so it is important at the start of your exercise program to be sensible and flexible about it. If you have been up all night and feel exhausted, then postpone the exercises until you have had a rest. If you feel energetic and full of purpose, then repeat the appropriate exercises a few more times; but take care not to overdo them as you will do more harm than good if you strain your muscles or overtire yourself. Observe your body rhythms and do not believe that an exercise must hurt to be beneficial. On the contrary, exercises should feel comfortable and make you feel good. Bear in mind that you have just been through one of the most exhausting and strenuous events of your life.

YOUR BODY
BEFORE AND AFTER
THE BIRTH

During pregnancy, you have undergone gradual changes to your physique, posture and emotions, yet within a matter of hours you have produced your baby and have started to experience a whole new range of changes. Some begin restoring your body to its former state, and others help you provide the necessary love, food and care for your baby.

The physical changes that take place are quite dramatic: naturally it does not take as long for the body to return to its pre-pregnancy state as it does to nurture a developing fetus from a single cell to an eight pound baby. In order to understand these postnatal physical changes and to see where exercise can help, it is helpful to familiarize yourself with your anatomy and to look at the way it is affected by both pregnancy and birth.

The pelvic girdle
The pelvic girdle is the bony framework at the bottom of your body. It is made up of four sets of bones; the first and most obvious are the big hip bones, which join in front at the symphysis pubis. They curve upwards to form two bony wings just beneath your waist and downwards to give you the bones you sit on. Wedged between these at the back is the sacrum (the base of the spine), joined to the hip bones at the sacroiliac joints. Finally there is the coccyx, all that remains of the human tail.

Like all the other joints of the body the pelvic joints are held together by ligaments. Normally little or no movement takes place in the pelvic joints, but during pregnancy, special tissue-softening hormones lead to the gradual softening and stretching of the body's ligaments which enable both the entrance and exit of the pelvis to increase in size as your baby passes through during labor.

Curving between the sacrum and the head are the twenty-four bones of the spine. If you put one hand on your symphysis pubis, and the other on your sacrum, you will see that the distance from back to front is not very great; in fact the internal diameter of the pelvis from back to front is only 10-12 cm (4-5 in). Usually your

The pelvic girdle

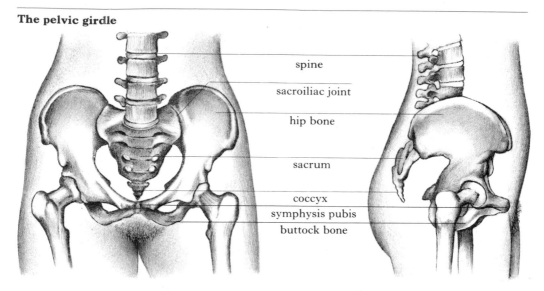

spine

sacroiliac joint

hip bone

sacrum

coccyx
symphysis pubis
buttock bone

pelvic organs – bladder, uterus and rectum – fit quite comfortably into this space, but by the end of your pregnancy the baby in the uterus makes things a very tight squeeze.

The ligaments

Ligaments are inelastic bands of connective tissue which help hold your joints together. During pregnancy the ligaments soften and stretch due to the influence of the hormones progesterone and relaxin, resulting in some relaxation in all the joints, not just the pelvic girdle. The effects of these changes can persist for up to five months after your baby is born, and may be felt as aching or sometimes pain, especially in the joints of your back, and the joints between your spine and pelvis (the sacroiliac joints). The joint in the front of your pelvis (the symphysis pubis) can give rise to problems as well.

The uterus

The uterus is a muscular bag which normally weighs less than 100 g (3.5 oz), and fits snugly into your pelvic girdle along with the other organs. By the end of your pregnancy the uterus alone weighs about 1 kg (2.2 lb).

Involution

Immediately after the birth your uterus can be felt through your soft abdominal wall just below the umbilicus. It is about the size it was at the fourth month of pregnancy. It immediately starts to contract down – the process known as involution – returning to its former size and position by six weeks. The contractions of involution may initially be felt as 'after pains', which will be more pronounced if you already have one or more children. Breastfeeding stimulates these contractions, which may feel like period pains or the discomfort felt in very early labour. Involution is entirely involuntary; it is a normal part of the reproductive process.

The blood forced out by your contracting uterus from the raw site of the placenta is called the lochia. It should be red for the

The pelvic organs

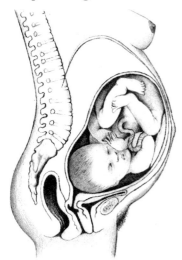
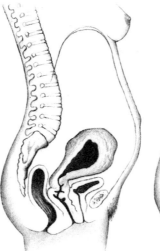
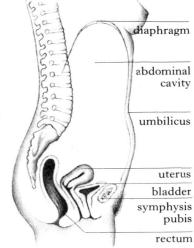

diaphragm

abdominal
cavity

umbilicus

uterus
bladder
symphysis
pubis
rectum

At the end of pregnancy
Because of your bulging
abdomen your posture alters,
and the organs are compressed.

Immediately after the birth
You will probably still look
about 6 months pregnant.

6 weeks after the birth
Your uterus should have
contracted down to its normal
shape, size and position.

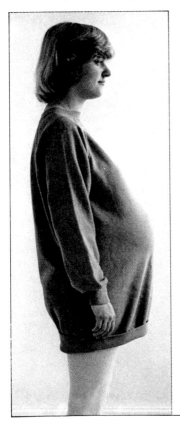

first few days, gradually changing to brown and finally disappearing between two to six weeks. You should report any large clots, sudden heavy loss or offensive smell to your doctor or midwife.

Within about two weeks of the delivery it is no longer possible to feel your uterus in your abdomen, as it has shrunk down into your pelvis (though it is still larger than normal). When you go for your postnatal check your doctor will examine you to make sure your uterus has fully contracted.

The pelvic floor

Holding everything in place underneath the pelvis is a hammock of muscle known as the pelvic floor, which is enormously stretched by childbirth. The pelvic floor muscles are divided into a deep and a superficial layer and have three openings: the urethra (from the bladder); the vagina (from the uterus); and the rectum and anus (from the bowel). The muscle fibres surround each of these openings in a figure eight, the front part looping round the vagina and urethra and the back part around the anus. The muscles are interconnected and work as one complete unit. The wedge of muscles between the vagina and the anus is known as the perineum. If you have an episiotomy to assist the safe delivery of your baby, this is usually where it will be.

The muscles making up the pelvic floor are quite small; they are held together by sheets of non-stretchy tissue called fascia. Normally most people are completely unaware of them, yet they are very important for health and comfort as they support the pelvic organs and prevent the bladder and bowel from leaking. (Strong pelvic floor muscles are also essential for an enjoyable sex life.)

During pregnancy the pelvic floor will have had to carry the increased weight of your baby and uterus; during the second stage of labor it will have thinned out and stretched open around your baby's head and body. It may also have been damaged by a tear, and many women experience acute pain in this area for several days.

If you have had stitches following a large tear or episiotomy,

The pelvic floor muscles

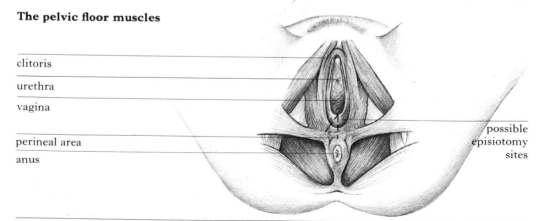

clitoris

urethra

vagina

perineal area

anus

possible episiotomy sites

you may need to take mild pain-killers for a while. The wound should be kept as clean and dry as possible by frequent bathing and changing of sanitary napkins. It may be recommended that heat treatment or ice is applied to the area to promote healing and relieve pain. At home, two to three minutes' massage with an ice-cube or five to ten minutes' gentle warmth with a hair dryer (set at its lowest heat), or with a reading lamp, can be soothing and give relief from the pain.

If you have had an episiotomy or tear it may help you overcome any anxieties you have about it if you look at it in a mirror after a few days. You will probably be surprised how well bonded the wound looks.

Three common problems

1 **Sitting down** Occasionally the post-episiotomy pain is so severe that some women are forced to feed their babies standing up! Sitting on a rubber ring or two folded pillows can prove help-ful by removing pressure from the area. Make sure you put your sorest part in the hole in the middle.

2 **Coughing, sneezing or laughing** As you cough a lot of pressure is exerted on your stitches, and it can feel as if they are bursting. It is much more comfortable if you remember to brace your pelvic floor muscles while you cough, sneeze, blow your nose or laugh (see page 52).

3 **Bowel movements** You will *not* tear your stitches if you have to strain to open your bowels. Support them with a folded sanitary towel to control the pain (see page 16).

If discomfort and pain in this area persist when you walk, sit, stand or make love, be sure to mention it to your doctor when you have your postnatal check-up: you should not have to put up with long-standing pain. If scar tissue is causing problems, discuss it with your physician or midwife.

Sexual problems

There is no "normal" time to resume sexual intercourse, although most women prefer to wait until the lochia is finished. You may feel desire as early as seven days or not for several weeks after your baby's birth (or even longer).

When you do both feel like trying intercourse, but you find it is very painful, stop and leave it for a few days. It may be that using a lubricating gel (available at any drugstore) would help your partner achieve a gentler penetration, or that adopting another position would make a difference to the pain in your vagina and breasts. If you both lie on your sides or you lie or sit above your partner, then you will be able to control his penetration and the pressure on your tender breasts.

Sex is not just a matter of physical comfort, of course, and you may find that your feelings towards your partner seem to change after the birth (see page 35). Guilt about this apparent change, fear of pain or damage to the perineum, anxiety about becoming pregnant again, or simply preoccupation with your baby can all affect your desire for sex. You may also feel flabby and unattractive. It is far better to talk these things through with your partner rather than maintain a martyred silence. After all, there are many other ways of reaching mutual satisfaction apart from actual intercourse.

If you are still finding intercourse painful or impossible, when you go for your postnatal check-up at about six weeks, do not be afraid to mention it. (This is also the time to discuss contraception if you have not done so already.) Your perineum should be checked for healing, the vaginal opening checked for size, the strength of your vaginal muscles tested, and your cervix examined to exclude the presence of a cervical erosion (ulcer) which could be a cause of pain during lovemaking. If your vaginal opening is found to be too tight, it can be treated – perhaps by gentle stretching. If you find that, far from a vagina which is too tight, you have been left feeling loose and floppy so that neither of you gets any pleasure from intercourse, you should also mention this. It may be that an intensive regime of pelvic floor exercises will cure this, but if not, then a minor surgical repair may be recommended to correct the problem.

Stress incontinence

Stress incontinence may have troubled you at the end of your pregnancy; more likely it is something which only developed after your baby was born. It is the uncontrollable leakage of urine from your bladder when you cough, sneeze, laugh or blow your nose, when you pick up something heavy, or perhaps run for a bus. Your pelvic floor exercise (see page 52) can be the answer to this problem. Practise this little tightening movement constantly: once a day is *not* enough. You should aim at four good contractions per hour. Initially you may have very poor sensation around the vagina but it will gradually return to normal and you will be able to feel these muscles working together, lifting inwards and upwards. Use the pelvic floor contraction while coughing or blowing your nose. As you breathe in to cough, quickly draw the pelvic floor in and up; hold it tightly braced until the cough is over, and only then relax.

Although stress incontinence is usually cured by correct and conscientious exercising, sometimes you may have such badly stretched internal ligaments or vaginal and urethral tissue that a small repair operation could be necessary. If after three months of honest exercising you are still leaking embarrassingly, return to your doctor for further help. If a repair is indicated, your gynecologist may prefer to wait until your family is complete before performing the operation.

Hemorrhoids

Hemorrhoids, or piles, are swollen varicose veins in your rectum and anus. Sometimes they appear in pregnancy, sometimes only after the baby is born – pushing in the second stage of labor can make them worse and they can be extremely painful, making sitting down truly uncomfortable. Once again, your pelvic floor exercise will help by improving the circulation in this sensitive area and therefore reducing the pain. An ice-cube gently held to the grape-like swelling can also give relief, and there are anesthetic and anti-inflammatory ointments and suppositories which your doctor can prescribe. It is also important to avoid any straining when you go to the bathroom.

The abdominal muscles

The first thing many mothers do after their delivery is to touch their stomachs and notice how flat they feel, yet how flabby. This is because the abdominal muscles which have been stretched round the uterus do not of course immediately return to their original shape – and will not properly without help.

The muscle layers

The abdominal wall consists of four layers of muscles. There are two superficial muscles – the Recti Abdominis – running straight up and down; two pairs of oblique muscles; and one pair of transverse muscles. This abdominal girdle joins down the mid-line, where a strip of fibrous tissue called the Linea Alba – normally about 1 cm ($\frac{1}{2}$ in) wide – can actually be seen on thin, muscular people. The abdominal muscles are weakest in the front, where the recti abdominis are only one layer deep. The other muscles overlap to form three layers at the sides.

How the muscles stretch

During pregnancy the abdominal muscles stretch around the growing uterus; a woman who normally measures about 33 cm (13 in) from breastbone to pubis can stretch to around 50 cm (20 in), while her waist might increase from 66 cm (26 in) to 101 cm (46 in)! As the body's ligaments soften during pregnancy, the Linea Alba also softens; in late pregnancy it is quite common for the two recti to separate above and below the umbilicus. Unless they are very thin, few women realize this is happening because this condition – known as diastasis recti – is completely painless. However, separation weakens the abdominal wall which may give rise to constant backache. It may seem strange that back pain can be brought about by weak front muscles, but that is the case; apart from holding your abdominal organs in place and giving you a waistline, the other role of the abdominal muscles is to support the back. That is why it is vitally important to begin

Changes in the abdominal muscles

linea alba

transverse abdominal

internal oblique

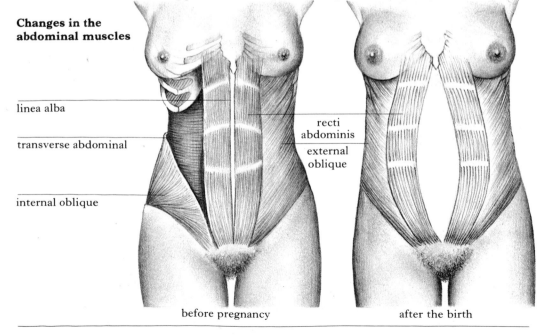

recti abdominis

external oblique

before pregnancy   after the birth

the program of exercises as soon as possible after the birth, to bring the abdominal muscles back to their former strength and tautness, so that you avoid difficulties with backache.

Multiple births

If you are carrying more than one baby you will inevitably feel more tired and uncomfortable towards the end of your pregnancy. Postnatally your abdominal muscles will be much weaker and the separation between the Recti will be much greater, so that it may take longer to reach full recovery. You will probably have to spend more time than mothers of single babies on the early stages of the exercise program, and be particularly careful not to increase fatigue by trying to do too much too soon.

Constipation

Some women suffer from constipation during pregnancy, while others become constipated following the birth of their babies. Some iron tablets are constipating and the hormones of pregnancy, which soften your ligaments, also relax your intestines so that they are not as efficient as they used to be at expelling their contents. Once your baby is born an additional factor comes into play – your abdominal muscles are now loose and floppy and give very poor support to the intestines.

Another cause of postnatal constipation is simply fear of straining or tearing stitches in the perineum. If this is the case, take two clean sanitary napkins with you into the bathroom – fold one in half and use it to press gently up against your stitches as you bear down to open your bowels.

If you are constipated it is very important to eat extra high-fiber foods, such as wholegrain bread, bran cereals, fresh fruit (do not peel your apples and pears), celery, cabbage and so on. You can add bran to your soups, stewed fruit, or yogurt – and be sure to drink extra fluid too. If, in spite of a sensible diet, you are still in trouble, ask your doctor to recommend a suitable laxative – you should not take anything which might affect your baby if you are breastfeeding.

The breasts

The breasts are neither muscle nor ligament; they are mainly fat with a small amount of glandular tissue. During pregnancy they will have enlarged so that your bra size may have increased substantially. By the end of your pregnancy some of the fat under the skin of the breasts will have been absorbed, the milk-producing glands will have grown and developed and you may have noticed the first few drops of colostrum – the substance that precedes true breast milk – being secreted.

Production of milk

After your baby is born the changing hormones cause the colostrum which has been produced in your breasts since mid-pregnancy gradually to change in composition until it becomes "true" milk between the third and fourth days. It is most beneficial for both mother and baby to nurse immediately after birth and often thereafter, as frequent nursing stimulates the milk supply, insuring adequate nutrition for even the fastest-growing baby. The practice of "rooming-in", available at most hospitals in this country, makes the establishment of breast-feeding easier by allowing mother and baby to find their own

Structure of the breasts

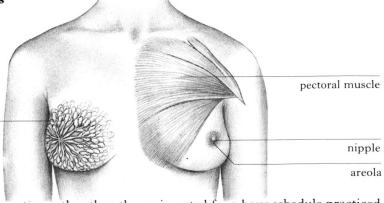

pectoral muscle

milk-producing glands

nipple

areola

routine rather than the regimented four-hour schedule practiced under the central nursery system.

As the breasts fill with milk they may feel firm, large and heavy. If frequent nursing has not been possible, they may become engorged and feel hot, hard and tender. Warm compresses and gentle hand expression will soften the breasts and help to start the flow. A nurse can demonstrate the technique and frequent nursing can insure the problem is quickly resolved.

If you are breastfeeding it is usually thought to be important to wear a well-supporting bra as the extra weight in your breasts may cause them to sag. Unlike muscle, breast tissue does not recover once stretched. However, although there are no exercises for the breasts themselves, it is certainly possible to improve the strength of the pectorals, their supporting muscles.

Breast toning exercises (see page 60) will not prevent your breasts from drooping, but they will help improve your posture, which is probably the most important factor in determining the position of your breasts on the chest wall. If you stand or sit with rounded shoulders, your breasts are much more likely to droop than if you are aware of your posture. Keep your back straight, lift your ribs and remember to keep your shoulders down and relaxed. Using the pectoral muscles vigorously will improve circulation and so may help lactation. For women with small breasts, developing the pectoral muscles enhances breast size.

The back, buttocks and breasts

After birth, it is extremely important to restore back and buttock muscles to their normal strength, as weakness here leads to poor posture and backache, which are so important a whole chapter has been devoted to them (see page 22).

The back and buttock muscles are made up of several layers, plus a great deal of fascia. The longest and most complicated muscle is the Erector Spinae, which runs from the sacrum and pelvic bones to the neck and skull, attaching on the way to many of the vertebrae, ribs and powerful ligaments of the spine. It not only causes movement but is also vital for maintaining good posture.

The muscles of your thighs and buttocks are among the most

The muscles of the back, buttocks and thighs

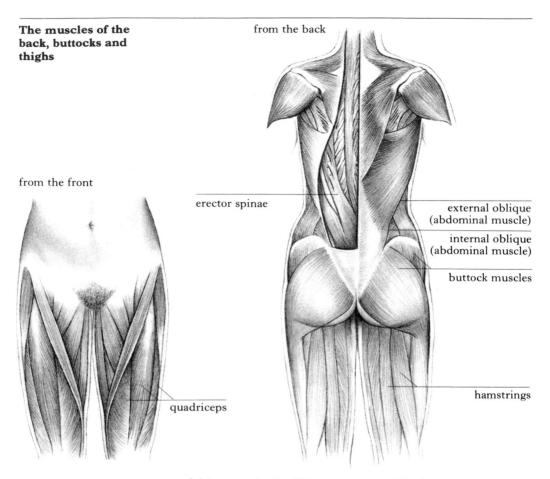

from the back

from the front

erector spinae

external oblique (abdominal muscle)

internal oblique (abdominal muscle)

buttock muscles

hamstrings

quadriceps

powerful in your body. They are responsible for the movements of the hips and knees and, together with the abdominal muscles, also help to maintain posture. The buttocks comprise a large mass of muscle covered in fascia and fat which produce movements of the hip.

The muscles of your legs do not change in pregnancy, although your legs may become heavier and be prone to swelling, especially if you suffer from edema (fluid retention). The muscles can however be strengthened and firmed by exercise, which will also improve the circulation and lessen the swelling.

Weight loss

After delivery you will have lost the weight of your baby, the amniotic fluid, and the placenta – probably about 3-5 kg (7-11 lb). You may lose an extra 1–1½ kg (2–3 lb) over the next few days as you excrete excess fluid from both tissues and extra blood volume. The uterus gradually shrinks from 1 kg (2.2 lb) to about 50-70 g (2-3 oz) during the next six weeks. However you will probably find you are still heavier than you were before you became pregnant. This difference is mostly stored fat and fluid.

Diet

If you are breastfeeding, some of this fat may be broken down to help produce breast milk and you may also be burning much of it up simply by doing the endless jobs involved in being a mother. However, just as it was during pregnancy, it is a myth that if you are breastfeeding you must eat for two. Dieticians advise that a breastfeeding mother only needs about 600-800 calories more per day than one who is bottlefeeding. Pay attention to the quality of your food, as well as the quantity, avoiding the "empty calories" contained in sweets, cakes and cookies. A well-balanced diet (including protein foods such as meat and fish or beans and other legumes, dairy foods, fruit, vegetables, fiber and complex carbohydrates) is vital for an adequate supply of breast milk. Always be careful about the amount of fat in your diet – butter, margarine, cheese, cream, fatty meat, oils and fried foods. Skimmed milk will give you all the nutrients you need with half the calories. You may find you are very thirsty, so take extra fluid, but if you are overweight remember that nearly all drinks except water contain calories.

If you are still over your ideal weight by the time your baby is about six months old, then adjust the quantity of your food intake while maintaining its quality and balance. Record your weight regularly (but not more than once a week) to ensure you are gradually losing your excess fat. If you are breastfeeding, do not attempt any crash diets as they may affect your health, energy and milk supply. However, there is nothing to restrict the bottlefeeding mother from dieting sensibly from the start. If, despite adequate diet and rest, you feel excessively tired and irritable, you may be anemic and iron supplements may be prescribed by your doctor.

Obesity

You may be one of those women who finds herself still in her maternity clothes months after her baby was born. You hear conflicting advice from well-meaning friends and relatives about diet; you don't want to affect your ability to breastfeed but you worry that your partner will no longer find you attractive if you do not lose weight soon. Sometimes you find yourself so miserable that you eat to console yourself, though you know that this is only making the problem worse.

It is important not to let your problem become an obsession which is far more tedious and offputting than the weight itself. Your first step should be to seek expert advice: go to your doctor and ask for a referral to a nutritionist. She will take your individual circumstances into consideration – your weight before pregnancy, your energy requirements, whether you are breastfeeding or not, your budget – and then advise you on what you can eat to lose weight safely and with certainty.

Secondly, try to borrow or buy some clothes that are loose fitting and comfortable, but which are not maternity clothes, so you are not mistakenly asked "When is it due?". Thirdly, remember that your partner has always found more than just your body attractive. His greatest wish will be to see you well and happy so that he can enjoy his new family.

POSTURE AND BACK CARE

Your posture

Your posture is the way you hold yourself upright; it can often tell the world how you feel. Everyone makes assumptions about people based on their posture – good posture is as important as a smile or an easy manner.

What is good posture? It is not only a matter of appearance but also of function – it should be efficient, comfortable and adaptable to the movements and positions used throughout the day. It is largely controlled by a reflex (subconscious) mechanism but is also considerably influenced by outside factors, such as emotions, neglected or damaged muscles and weight change. In pregnancy it is also affected by the softening of ligaments and the resulting joint laxity. Fortunately most postural faults can be corrected in a young, healthy person, but if they are not, they may go on to produce joint changes, sometimes leading to arthritis and long-standing discomfort.

How pregnancy influences posture

During your pregnancy three main factors contribute to the adjustment (and often deterioration) of your posture. The first is the hormonal influence, causing your ligaments to soften; the second is the gradual increase and changed distribution of your weight; the third is your self image and emotions – your feelings about your shape and the developing baby. Unless you are aware of these gradual changes you may find that after your baby is born, you still look several months pregnant. Your body's postural reflex has over-compensated and may be "stuck" in the stance of pregnancy. You will need to re-educate your muscles to correct it.

Assessing your posture

To help you assess your posture, you will need to be aware of the common postural problems of the pregnant woman. As the baby grows in her uterus, a combination of the forward movement of her center of gravity and stretched, weak, abdominal muscles most commonly cause her to adapt by hollowing her lower spine, pushing her knees back, rounding her shoulders and poking her chin forward. Her softened ligaments allow an unusual flexibility of the spine, and if she is not aware that her posture is faulty, her

back muscles eventually shorten as her abdominal muscles stretch, with extra stresses placed on the ligaments and bones of the spine and pelvis. The usual result is backache.

After the birth, your perineal stitches (or in the case of a Caesarean section, abdominal stitches) may be so uncomfortable when you first get up to walk that your whole body sags forward and you shuffle along anxiously with your legs together. Holding an abnormal position because of pain, or the fear of it, is very tiring. You can be certain that your cut is soundly stitched and that 'standing tall' as described below, and taking a gentle walk, will improve not only your posture and appearance, but also your circulation and comfort.

Correcting your posture

1 Look at yourself sideways in a long mirror, or ask a friend to check you. Stand as tall as you can: imagine someone has grabbed a tuft of hair from the top of your head and is pulling it upwards.
2 Tighten your buttocks and pull in your abdominal muscles as you tilt your whole pelvis backwards (your pubic bone should move forwards and up as this happens).
3 Move your feet about 60 cm (12 in) apart and feel the weight on their outside edges.
4 Take a deep breath and expand your ribs upwards and outwards, with your arms hanging loosely but rolled slightly outwards.
5 Now relax your breathing to a slow, deep rhythm that is natural to you.

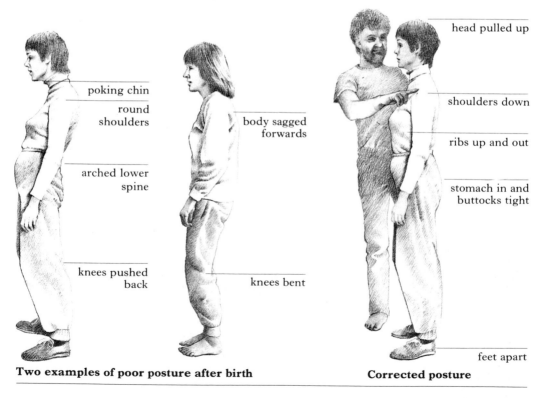

poking chin
round shoulders

arched lower spine

knees pushed back

body sagged forwards

knees bent

head pulled up

shoulders down

ribs up and out

stomach in and buttocks tight

feet apart

Two examples of poor posture after birth   **Corrected posture**

Feel your new posture; note the muscles that are working to hold it for you, especially your abdominal and buttock muscles. It may feel extremely odd and unnatural at first, but be reassured by your mirror image or your critical friend that it has now improved.

Try to visualize that your muscles are made of a special type of elastic which has been overstretched but which, with use, has the power to rejuvenate. Now feel the muscles you are using to hold your new, corrected posture, and see if you can continue to hold them braced as often as possible throughout the day while you stand, sit or walk. At first this will be a conscious effort, but gradually the muscles themselves will adapt by becoming shorter and more elastic, and you will no longer need to think about them as they hold your improved position. Try to introduce your new awareness of good posture into everything you do, whether it is working or resting. As well as your baby, of course, it could be one of the long term benefits of childbirth.

Other ways to improve your posture

1 When you sit down in a chair to feed your baby or to relax, make sure you choose one that is the right height and depth, and which gives good support. The ideal chair is one with a firm back support into which you push your buttocks, and a seat which provides support for your thighs while still allowing your knees to relax at right angles and your feet to rest flat on the floor. You may find it even more comfortable to put a cushion behind your waist. When you are nursing, lie your baby on a pillow on your lap and rest one or both feet on a footstool (or perhaps a pile of telephone directories or other large books). Both these aids will help raise your baby up towards your breasts, preventing the need to lean too far forward.

2 When you lie down to rest, make sure you are comfortable and

Good feeding position

Bad feeding position

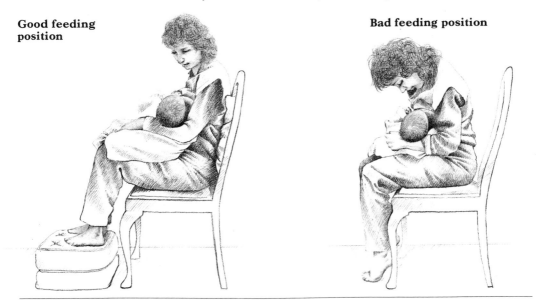

that your vulnerable back is not strained in any way. If you like to lie on your back, put a pillow under your thighs to help flatten the hollow in your spine.

Lying on your front is an excellent position for relieving the pain of perineal stitches, hemorrhoids and backache. Make certain you put one or even two pillows under your waist, so that your pelvis is raised and your back flattened. You will probably also find it more comfortable to have a pillow or two under your head and shoulders, so that your enlarged breasts are free from pressure. (If you have had a Caesarean section you will not be able to use this position immediately, but in two to three weeks you too will be able to enjoy it.) Rest in this position several times a day if you can. It has probably been impossible to lie on your stomach for months, so enjoy it now.

3 Shoes also have an important influence on your posture. Those with a $2\frac{1}{2}$-5 cm (1-2 in) heel are ideal as they lessen the tendency to hollow the lower back. It is important not to wear very high heels too often, as they will throw your weight even further forward and exaggerate the curve of your spine.

Back care

Back problems are among the most common complaints of pregnancy and during the first few months after the birth. As has already been described, during pregnancy hormones cause the ligaments of the pelvis and spine to soften and stretch, so that poor posture, faulty lifting, excessive weight gain or a previous back problem may then all contribute to strain on the joints of the spine or pelvis, and cause backache or pain. The joint laxity caused by the softened ligaments may persist for five months after your baby is born, so extra care must be taken during this entire time. Refer back to the hints on good posture given earlier, as well as those given opposite, and remember that the best treatment for back problems is to prevent them.

The sacroiliac and lower back ligaments

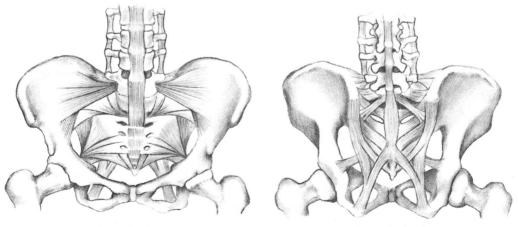

from the front   from the back

Preventing back damage

1 When you sit down, make sure your bottom is pressed well into the back of the chair; and perhaps use a pillow to hold your back upright.

Do not slump or slouch in a soft chair.

2 As you roll over or get out of bed, avoid twisting or turning with your knees apart. First tighten your abdominal muscles, bend your knees and roll onto your side; then push yourself up into the sitting position with your arms, swing both your legs over the bed, knees together, and stand up.

3 When you are standing to do household chores, put one foot up on a low stool or two or three telephone directories, or rest one foot on the bottom shelf of a cupboard, letting you use your back more comfortably.

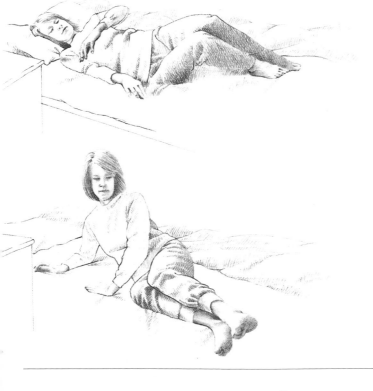

4 When lifting a toddler or a heavy weight such as a bucket full of soaking diapers, pull your abdominal muscles in, tuck in your buttocks and brace your pelvic floor. Keeping your spine straight, bend your legs to kneel or squat down, bring the weight close to your body, and, using your stronger thighs to bear the weight, slowly rise to standing. This will protect the much smaller muscles and ligaments of your back, and is also, incidentally, an excellent way of toning flabby thigh muscles. If you are lifting your baby in a bassinet, have the head nearest to you – this will put less strain on your back. Never lift when bending or twisting to the side. When pushing or pulling a weight, such as moving furniture, make sure your knees are bent and mobile.

5 Remember to protect your back by doing low household chores, such as making the bed, bathing your baby or dressing your toddler, on your knees. Squat or kneel to pick things up off the the floor.

6 If you are vacuuming or sweeping, move your weight forwards and backwards over your front leg, keeping your back straight; avoid the risky twisting movement while bending forward.

7 When choosing a carrier, carriage or stroller for carrying or transporting your baby, think of your back (see page 64). Choose a carrier which holds your baby centrally (front or back) and which is adjustable so that you can raise your baby up as far as is comfortable to you both. Choose a carriage or stroller that has handles that are high enough to push it without stooping forward.

8 Make sure the surface on which you change your baby is at the right height for you. About waist level is ideal in the early months, before your baby has learnt to roll. Then perhaps you can progress to changing him sitting on the floor with your legs astride and back kept straight.

9 If your bed is very soft, it will help if you slide a bed board between the mattress and the box spring, or put the mattress on the floor.

Coping with backache

In spite of your best endeavors, you may still find that backache is a problem in the postnatal period. Indeed many women experience it during pregnancy. When you noticed that first gnawing ache or twinge of pain after your baby was born, you sincerely hoped that it would pass, along with some of the other transient discomforts you have felt as a new mother. It may indeed go away; on the other hand, it may persist, leaving you in intermittent or sometimes constant pain, so that you are practically immobilized, finding that you are unable to function normally until it passes.

Where backache occurs

By far the commonest site of this ache or pain after birth is the sacroiliac joint, where the spine joins the pelvis on either side. It is normally felt over the joint, (which lies immediately under one of the two dimples on either side of the spine), becoming acute on pressure or when twisting the lower spine. The pain may radiate into the whole buttock, and there is sometimes associated tenderness at the front over the pubic bone. The backache experienced can be constant, and there may be pain down the leg. Walking short distances is often reasonably comfortable, but the pain will then usually get progressively worse. It may be difficult to bear weight on the affected leg (such as when climbing stairs), there is little relief felt after lying down, and you may feel stiff after a period of sitting.

Intervertebral disc damage

Very severe pain may be caused by damage to a disc between the vertebrae of the spine, although this is extremely rare compared to backache due to the combination of softened ligaments, poor posture and excess weight. This may cause lumbago (incapacitating pain in the lower back) or sciatica (pain along the sciatic nerve – through the buttock, back of the thigh and calf and into the foot); the pain will be worst when sitting, coughing and bending forwards – which will be restricted. Lying down usually relieves the symptoms. The treatment for disc problems is usually bed-rest, so if you have had a history of back problems, or feel that yours may fit this description, then retire to bed and ask for further medical advice.

RELIEVING LOW BACK PAIN

Advice has already been given on how to protect your back, but if you experience persistent backache, there are several ways to alleviate and often cure sacro-iliac pain. If you have any history of back trouble, consult with a doctor before performing these maneuvers, and stop doing them immediately if you experience increased back pain. The same applies to the other exercises in the book.

One method of relieving low back pain is pelvic rocking, as described on page 84 under the exercise called "Cat Arch".

If you are unable to kneel down on all fours when your back is aching, try the exercise while sitting or even standing up. If you experience back pain in bed, roll onto your side and, with your knees bent, rock your pelvis gently backwards and forwards.

If this does not help, or if your pain is acute and keeps you from walking, then lie on the floor and try one of the following maneuvers. (The examples given are for right-sided pain; reverse them if the pain is on your left.)

KNEE TO SHOULDER PULLS
Bend your right leg up (as shown), holding it around the knee with your right hand, and with your left hand cupping the heel of the right foot, pull the right heel towards your groin. Keeping your shoulders flat and left leg straight, press the bent leg further up towards the right shoulder, as far as it will comfortably go. Slowly relax. Repeat several times, then, keeping your knees together, roll onto your side, push up onto all fours, and stand carefully, keeping your back straight.

TWISTING ROCKS

Lie on your back on the floor. Bend your right leg and hook your right toes under the outside of your left calf, rolling your right knee towards the left. Now take your left arm across your body so that your left hand holds your right hip. Rock gently in this position; then roll back to the starting position. Relax slowly. Repeat several times. Again take care when you stand up – knees together to roll onto your side, then push onto all fours, and keep your back straight as you rise to stand.

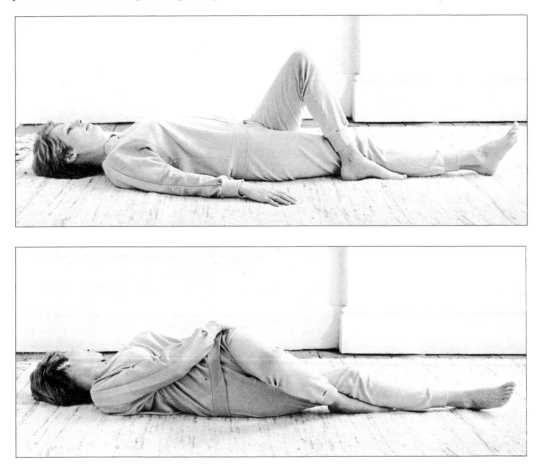

Seeking medical advice   If your backache continues, as a first-aid measure try wearing a panty girdle to support the aching joints. It may give very good relief and will not weaken your abdominal muscles as long as you remember to use them to hold yourself in. If your backache begins to affect your ability to cope with your family, then do not hesitate to seek medical advice. Treatment may be as simple as one dramatic manipulation, or you may be advised very firmly to take a period of rest flat on your back. Whatever is needed, you must try to tackle the problem now, however inconvenient or impossible it may seem. Back problems have a habit of recurring as acute and crippling episodes or chronic, nagging aches.

YOUR FEELINGS
AFTER THE BIRTH

Emotional changes

No matter how intensely you looked forward to the birth of your baby, or how much you expected that the rewards of motherhood would compensate for your loss of freedom or job satisfaction, it is as well to be prepared for a tiring, tense and possibly traumatic first few weeks. Women change and develop emotionally as much as physically during pregnancy and the early days of motherhood.

In the same way that the enlarging uterus and softening ligaments of pregnancy trouble some women during the gestation of their babies – so the change in lifestyle from independence to motherhood can also prove painful for some. In fact, becoming a parent is one of life's most important revolutions, and is often described as a "life crisis", similar to the upheaval involved in marriage, bereavement, changing or losing a job, or moving. However, if you are prepared for some of the feelings and problems which can occur after your baby is born you may be able to cope with them more easily.

Immediate feelings after the birth

The way you feel in the first few hours following delivery can vary enormously. You may be euphoric, flat, detached, tearful, overjoyed, or disappointed. A lot will depend on the length and type of labor you have just experienced. Naturally you are going to feel more tired if your labor has been long and painful, especially if you missed out on more than one night's sleep. You may have set yourself all sorts of goals to achieve in labor, and feel a failure because, instead of an active, natural childbirth you ended up with Demerol, an epidural, an episiotomy and a forceps delivery. You may have set your heart on a golden haired daughter and have got instead a dark haired son with forceps marks on his face, who looks very much like your least favorite relative. Some women fall in love with their babies instantly, but many others have a detached feeling about them – their overriding reaction being a desire to roll over and go to sleep.

Apart from the initial fatigue that follows labor, tremendous changes in the hormonal balance may also affect the emotions.

The hormonal changes that enable the breasts to produce milk may also cause overwhelming shifts in mood.

Something you may not have been expecting is missing the presence of your baby within your body. Even though you have been longing for your balloon-like shape to disappear, you may feel empty and lonely after your baby is born and miss his movements intensely. (Your baby will almost certainly feel lonely too.) Another strange and probably completely unexpected feeling is a sense of anticlimax. Labor, which is often seen as the "grand finale" of pregnancy before you return to normal, is actually the "overture" to a completely new life-style.

"Baby blues"

"Baby blues" can be another distressing reaction. They usually creep up on you between two days and a week after the birth, or even later. Emotions that go up have to come down. If the first 48 hours of your role as mother has floated by in a haze of pink cloud, it can be a shock then to experience tearfulness, depression and feelings of helplessness. Little things may trigger bouts of crying – maybe your partner arrives five minutes late for visiting time; or a nurse speaks to you abruptly. You may also notice violent mood swings, one minute feeling intense surges of mother love, and yet the next being driven to desperation because the baby is crying. The blues may simply overwhelm you because you hate hospital routines, your bed is uncomfortable, the food tasteless, your stitches hurt, and you feel homesick.

Early days at home

Once you are home with your baby the most devastating discovery for the first-time mother may be that you are on duty 24 hours a day, seven days a week – there is no let up. First-timers have the additional burden of having to learn how to be mothers and fathers – parents having a second or subsequent baby have learned this lesson and birth is probably not such an overwhelming experience.

Many women who held down responsible jobs feel failures because they cannot cope domestically – the chores pile up and they are still in their bathrobes by mid-afternoon. Breastfeeding and bottlefeeding both present problems, although you are more likely to feel a failure if you cannot breastfeed.

Catching up with sleep

Most young women are used to an uninterrupted night's sleep of eight to nine hours, and it can take several months until they get used to their new way of life and for the intense fatigue to disappear. Your motto at first should be, "sleep when the baby sleeps", which is easy after a first baby, but not quite so easy if you already have older children. If you cannot fit in an hour or two's sleep during the day, make the most of little catnaps whenever you can. Rest and relax, using the simple relaxation drill given on page 40, and make sure that feeding times are restful and relaxing too: put your feet up or curl up on your side on your bed. Make up your mind that for a while you do not need a spotlessly clean house; this is something that your partner can help with. If cooking is a problem for both of you, convenience foods or take-out meals are worth the extra expense for a while.

Finally there will be days when rest is more important to you than exercises. Don't worry if you are unable to fit the exercises in every day, and don't exercise at 11.30 pm at night when you are dropping with fatigue.

Crisis measure

If you feel that you are so completely drained of energy you cannot go on any longer, a useful tip is to go to bed as soon as you have eaten supper – say at 7 pm – and sleep until your baby wakes for a feeding. Ask your partner to bring the baby to you in bed; let him change the diaper – if necessary – halfway through the feed; then, when your baby is full of food and drops off to sleep, snuggle back into your covers and do the same, until the next feeding.

Anxiety and stress

Anxiety is an emotion which may constantly plague you during those early weeks – feeding, changing, sleeping all seem fraught with uncertainties. You may reach the stage when you feel compelled to telephone your partner begging him to come home and relieve you. He is your link with the outside world and you need his support. Some parents try to continue their lives as if nothing had happened, determined that the baby should in no way alter their cosy twosome – but it is practically impossible initially to be a perfect wife and mother simultaneously.

Your relationship with your partner

First time childbirth often disrupts a marriage in a way which can be totally unexpected – after all, a twosome which increases by 50 per cent to become a threesome is no longer the same, and there is bound to be a period of adjustment before the new situation is accepted. You may find you feel very dependent, and this need for support will continue for a time after the baby is born. You will be constantly preoccupied with the baby – will certainly feel very tired, and will possibly be depressed too – so that you may be unable to give your husband the care and attention he needs. You may find you both have unspoken fears about sex; you may not feel any desire for a while; he may be frightened of hurting you.

If you both decide before the birth that initially it will be *your* job to breastfeed your baby and rest if necessary, and his job to care for you both by taking on as much of the shopping, cooking and cleaning as he can manage, the early weeks will be much easier for all of you, and your relationship with each other will become much more of a partnership and therefore much more serene; whereas, if you desperately try to cope with everything *and* the baby, relations can be strained. Either way, fathers need to be involved from the beginning and communication is the key, so try and talk it through.

The older child

Another relationship which may change following the birth of a new baby is the one you have with your older children. Many parents worry and feel guilty before the birth of a second baby, particularly if there is a small age gap between the two children. They feel that perhaps they are being unfair to their firstborn, displacing him while he is still a baby.

Toddlers may show their jealousy by reverting to babyish habits – waking at night and forgetting their toilet training. They may not show their animosity to the baby directly, but will become "difficult" in their attempts to capture your interest. Even if there is a gap of many years, older children can show their anxiety and fear of being displaced in your affection by becoming truculent and untidy. It is difficult for firstborn children to appreciate that all children in a family are loved, and only time, plus your continued reassurance, will show them that they mean as much to you as their rival. Of course life has to continue, and chores have to be done – but many early relationship problems can happily be dealt with by touching and cuddling and *showing* each other that although the pattern of interaction has changed, affection and love are still there.

Preventing loneliness

Loneliness may be something you never experienced before your first baby was born. It is not until you are actually home – alone with your baby – that you might suddenly feel very isolated and miss adult conversation and company.

To avoid this, it is a good idea to exchange telephone numbers with some of the other expectant mothers in your prenatal class when you get to the end of your course, so that even if you are the first among your own friends or family to have a baby you will still be able to communicate with someone who appreciates how difficult those early weeks can be. The telephone can be a lifeline, even though it is not the same as human company.

Ask your midwife or doctor if they know of someone who has recently had a baby and who lives nearby; start conversations with other mothers when you visit the pediatrician or the park, and ask if they know of a "Mother and Baby Club". La Leche League has support groups for breastfeeding mothers, and many childbirth education groups sponsor mother-baby discussion groups. Remember that you are not the only new mother who is feeling so alone, and that probably most of the women you see in the supermarket and in the street with tiny babies are feeling the same way.

Postnatal depression

Most women will pass safely through the postnatal period with nothing more than a mild attack of the blues to bother them. But for some, a more severe form of emotional upset – postnatal depression – can become a long lasting, trying condition. It does not necessarily begin immediately after the baby is born, indeed it may be several weeks or months before it occurs, but its effect on both mother and family is shattering.

Symptoms of depression

Most postnatally depressed women complain of extreme exhaustion – not just the normal postnatal fatigue but something much more intense and continuous. Sadness and weepiness, a sense of inadequacy, tension and anxiety, irrational fears – these are all symptoms of this very common disorder. Some women complain of physical symptoms too – palpitations, dizziness, aching all over, an inability to sleep in spite of their tiredness, or a complete loss of libido (sexual interest). Sometimes a woman will complain of loss of appetite and will lose weight; yet other women will feel the need to go on frequent eating binges, putting on excessive weight instead of losing it. Women suffering from postnatal depression are often very irritable and short tempered and can experience terrifying moments when they really hate their children and feel a desperate impulse to harm them.

Feelings of aggression

You may have thought that your baby would sleep for 20 hours each day, only waking every so often for a feeding, so that you would have plenty of time for yourself. It is quite a shock to realize that even a two-week-old baby wants a social life and can stay awake for hours on end needing constant entertainment, driving you, meanwhile, to distraction. All normal parents will admit to terrifying moments when their baby pushes them to the brink of violence. Thankfully most of us step back from the brink, horrified by our feelings. Try not to feel too guilty about them; instead learn to recognize the signs, counter them with the crisis relaxation techniques given later on page 42 and find someone sympathetic in whom you can confide.

Dealing with depression

It is useless to tell a depressed woman to 'pull herself together' – she cannot do it. At a time when she feels she should be glowing with happiness and contentment, enjoying her new baby and family and coping with all the chores as efficiently as before her pregnancy, she finds herself in a slough of despondency.

Fortunately postnatal depression is now recognized much more frequently by doctors – and by mothers and their families too. It can be treated and women can be helped over this unpleasant period. Psychotherapy and/or anti-depressants may be used with good results. Some medications may be harmful to the breastfed baby; however, forced weaning may make the depression worse. The relative risks and benefits of any treatment should be considered by the prescribing physician in consultation with the couple. Talking to people about your feelings can also help enormously – your doctor or midwife, partner, relatives, childbirth educator, friends with older children – they will all understand and will help you realize that emotional upset is a common part of childbirth for some people, and, for the vast majority of us, can be dealt with swiftly.

Getting back to normal

The passing of time soon brings its compensations. The early weeks of constant caring gradually change when you see that first dazzling smile, when your baby "talks" back to you, and follows your movements around the room. Suddenly your baby is beginning to learn to socialize and you realize that normal life goes on outside the confines of parenthood, and there will be moments which you will treasure and which will remain with you even when your "baby" has begun to earn his own living!

At the end of the first three months the continuous hard physical work of caring for a new baby begins to be worth it – and both you and your partner will be glad to be parents after all.

THE IMPORTANCE
OF RELAXATION

During pregnancy your preparation for labor may have included learning relaxation techniques which help the body to cope with stress and work more efficiently. Even if you produce a large family, the total number of hours spent in labor during a lifetime is tiny, but the lessons learned in your prenatal classes can be readily applied to your life in general, and especially to those early days and weeks following birth.

Babies are born knowing instinctively how to relax; you will feel your own baby's deep relaxation when you hold him or her close to your body. You know how to relax too; every night when you drift into sleep the muscles of your body stop working and relax. Even without sleep you know how to relax: when you lie on the beach or in your back yard, soaking up the summer sun, your body comfortably supported, your muscles have no need to work and they relax. Faced with a stressful situation, however, you become tense – and your body will always react in the same way, regardless of the cause. Even babies respond to stress – pain, discomfort, loneliness, the fear of being dropped, or anger at not being fed.

The effects of stress

The stresses and strains we experience as we pass through childhood and adolescence to reach adult life produce muscle tensions which can give rise to postural distortions; raised tense shoulders, clenched fists, jaws clamped tightly together, pressed lips, furrowed forehead, and shallow rapid respiration. Mental turmoil often leads to physical tension and the vicious circle is established: the body reacts to the anxieties felt within by hunching, clenching, tightening, and gritting; this leads to aches and pains and more emotional distress. This reaction to stress is one of your body's primitive reflexes. You sense danger, and at once your muscles tense, ready to fight or run away. Other responses include sweating, pallor, pounding heart, dry mouth and faster, deeper respiration.

During pregnancy, labor and delivery stand before you rather

like the highest mountain of a range; once you have climbed it and reached its peak (the moment of birth) you imagine that the descent to new parenthood will be easy. As we have seen, you may in fact be totally unprepared for the reality of the early days and weeks of your new baby's life. Tension and fatigue seem to increase hourly; when your baby wakes for the fourth time one night your body reacts by producing the primitive stress response. You try to pacify him with tight, raised shoulders, anxiety and tiredness wrinkling your face – and a coiled spring of tension within you that may make you want to shake the wretched child back to sleep.

Reciprocal relaxation

Fortunately there is a very useful law of the body called reciprocal relaxation which can help you move away from the tense, hunched posture invoked by stress. While one group of muscles works to perform a movement, the opposite group has to relax. This is a physiological fact which you can use to help yourself. · For example, to bring ease and comfort to tightly clenched teeth, you can work the muscles which oppose the upward pull on your jaw. Try this: Clench your teeth. Then, with your lips just together, drag the lower jaw down – stop doing it and then notice the new position of your teeth, slightly apart. Your jaws are now relaxed.

The technique of 'simple relaxation'

Picture your reaction to the extreme stress of fear – a bomb explosion. Your shoulders are up, arms pulled into your sides, elbows bent and hands clenched, legs ready to run, body crouched forward, chin tucked into your chest, your face distorted. The following sequence of movements – a technique known as 'simple relaxation' – is the direct opposite to those your body makes to achieve the tension posture. Because of the law of reciprocal relaxation, following each individual movement, tense parts of your body will *always* become relaxed. Bit by bit you can take your body away from the posture of tension to the position of ease and relaxation.

Lie down comfortably on your back with your head and thighs supported by pillows.

1 Shoulders Pull your shoulders towards your feet – then stop pulling. Register the new position of ease in your mind – your shoulders are relaxed.

2 Arms Push your elbows out and open – stop pushing when you feel your position to be comfortable; register this position, your arms are relaxed.

3 Hands Let them rest comfortably on your thighs or tummy. Stretch the fingers so that they are long and straight; stop. Notice their new position – loosely curled and supported and relaxed.

4 Hips Tighten your buttocks and press your knees out sideways. Stop doing it – and notice the relaxed sensation in your hips.

5 Knees Lift your heels; stop doing it – and register the comfortable feeling in your knees and thighs.

6 Feet Press your feet away from your face. Stop doing it – and notice comfortable feet dangling on the ends of your legs.

7 Body Press your body into the support behind you; stop doing it – and register the pleasant sensation of relaxation in your abdomen.

8 Head Press your head into the support behind it – stop pressing – and notice how this movement has relaxed your neck and upper shoulders. (If you want to try this while sitting in a chair and your head is not supported, let it tilt forward slightly till it reaches a comfortable position.)

9 Face (a) your jaw: drag your lower jaw down; stop doing it – then notice the pleasant feeling of comfort that you have when your upper and lower sets of teeth are resting slightly apart.

(b) your mouth: stretch your lips sideways in a little smile, pout your lips forwards very quickly and then notice the pleasing sensation of soft warm lips just lightly touching each other.

(c) your eyes: your lids are resting comfortably over your eyes. You may even want to close them.

(d) your forehead: imagine that someone is stroking it and smoothing away the lines of tension.

Relaxing your jaw
Clenched teeth (right) often accompany tension. To relax your jaw, drag it down keeping your lips touching (center); then stop and let your teeth rest slightly apart (far right).

Breathing for relaxation

Because the way you breathe is affected by stress, altering your respiration is one of the easiest ways of inducing relaxation. You tend to breathe out as you relax: imagine your reaction to finding a lost purse with the next two weeks' food money in it – you sigh with relief and relax. If you use this response to deal with the many problems large and small which crop up continuously during parenthood, they can often be resolved painlessly. Breathe out and relax at the beginning of a feeding if you feel the needle-like pain from a sore nipple. Breathe out and relax when you realize that you have run out of disposable diapers. Breathe out and relax when your toddler unravels a completely new roll of toilet paper or empties the contents of his pot on the floor.

Use your breathing to increase the depth of your relaxation. Make it slow, calm and quiet. Concentrate on the outward breath – empty your chest – pause – and then let only as much air into your lungs as you need at that particular moment – do not force more and more air into your chest.

The beauty of 'simple relaxation' is that it always works – day or night – whatever your position (sitting, standing, lying), and whatever you are doing, (washing, feeding the baby, waiting for a bus). It is not always necessary to lie down in a darkened room surrounded by silence to be able to relax. You can take your hunched shoulders away from their tense position by simply moving them in the opposite direction.

Using simple relaxation

It is not necessary to run through the complete checklist of movements every time. Your shoulders, arms, hands and face are usually the first parts of your body to respond to stress – recognize the tension in them and release it by adjusting the stress-induced posture.

Whenever your baby is sleeping, experiment with several comfortable positions to use to rest, doze or sleep yourself. Feeding time gives you a wonderful opportunity to practice relaxation, for tension is catching; if you start nursing your baby while sitting uncomfortably, your back will begin to ache, you may be scared to move in case your baby stops suckling, you will become tense and long for the feeding to finish. In turn, your baby will sense this and will become disturbed and restless. Anxiety at the beginning of a feeding can delay the "let down" reflex which makes the milk-producing glands release the milk in your breasts. Use your relaxation to overcome this. Always make sure you are comfortable, close your eyes (if it helps) and consciously run through the body movements to give you complete relaxation.

Many mothers find it hard to get back to sleep once they have been disturbed by their baby at night; use your relaxation technique and slow calm breathing to help you float into sleep again. Relaxation is a valuable tool, always there for you to use during crises. If you learn it now it will be a lifelong legacy of childbirth.

Crisis measures

For those difficult moments when you reach breaking point, try this emergency relaxation measure.

Breathe out – then breathing naturally:

Face Smooth away worry lines – teeth apart.

Shoulders Down – stop – feel it.

Hands Long stretched fingers – stop – feel it.

Relaxing feeding positions

Left: Sit cross-legged on the floor with your back supported against a wall. Raise your baby by placing a pillow across your knees. Above: Lie on your side with your baby alongside you. Support your head and shoulders with two pillows and place another between your legs.

Comfortable relaxation positions

1 Lie on your front with a pillow under your hips. This position is particularly useful for the immediate postnatal period when you may have uncomfortable stitches.

2 Lie flat on your back with legs apart and palms upwards. Support your head with a pillow and place another under your knees.

3 An alternative to the above position is to raise your legs by resting your feet on a low stool or coffee table, with one pillow placed under your heels and another under your head.

4 You can relax in the middle of doing the chores for a few minutes by sitting at a table with your knees wide apart and feet flat on the floor, resting your head on your arms.

It is helpful to relax for five to ten minutes after you have completed your daily postnatal exercise sessions. The positions suggested in the Daily Program (pages 62, 89 and 112) are only given as guides; you could use whichever position described here seems most comfortable at the time.

EASY RELAXATION EXERCISES

UNCURLING

Stand up and bend forward so that your shoulders and arms hang heavily. Stay there, resting and breathing quietly. Slowly uncurl, bringing your body upwards. When you are straight stand still for a moment, breathing quietly. (If this exercise should make your back ache, try it sitting in a chair with your knees wide apart.)

SHOULDER CIRCLING

(This exercise can be done standing or sitting.) Circle your shoulders backwards, first one, then the other and then both together. Finish with them both down in a relaxed position.

ARM STRETCHING

S-T-R-E-T-C-H your arms as high as you can above your head; then stop and relax. You can do this stretching movement sitting down, standing up or lying down on your bed.

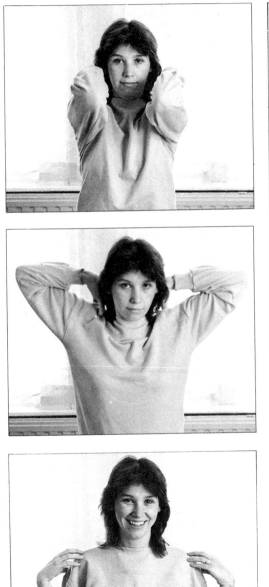

GETTING STARTED

EXERCISES
0 TO 6 WEEKS

First thoughts on exercise

Whether you had a long or short, easy or difficult labor, probably the last thing you will feel like doing immediately after your baby is born is to begin your postnatal exercises. Don't worry – you do not need to start a vigorous program immediately; there are a few simple movements though that will make you feel more comfortable.

Some women may have little or no discomfort, while others will notice heavy legs, a sore throbbing perineum or possibly backache. For those who have had a Caesarean section there may be intense burning pain over and around the line of the incision. Whatever your type of delivery, you will probably notice that every time you try to change your position during the first few hours, there will be a flow of blood from the vagina. Because of this you may, mistakenly, feel nervous of moving, let alone beginning your exercises. If you have stitches in your pelvic floor or abdomen, you may also be worried that they will come apart if you move too energetically. However, you can be quite sure that the exercises given in the first part (0-48 hours) of this section are not only safe but essential for your speedy recovery and you can even do the first four while still in the delivery room.

Make the most of your few days away from domestic chores; rest when you can, but try to fit in a few exercises three times a day. When you get home try to do them a minimum of twice a day. All the exercises in the first section, except for the first two, should be continued at home.

Being careful

Once you feel you are able to start the slightly harder exercises there are a few important rules to observe:
1 Never exercise to the point of pain or exhaustion.
2 Stop if you feel nauseated, dizzy or faint.
3 Learn to listen to your body so that you do not inadvertently strain your weak muscles.
4 Don't exercise last thing at night when you are feeling tired, or if you are ill.

A warning

There are two exercises which should *never* be attempted during this postnatal period; they are:
1 Lying flat on your back with both legs straight on the floor, and then trying to lift them together.
2 Lying flat on your back with both legs straight and attempting to sit up.
While both of these exercises might be acceptable for healthy young athletes in training, they are totally unsuitable and potentially dangerous for recently delivered women whose abdominal muscles and back ligaments are frail and easily damaged.

Breathing and exercise

Some exercise experts insist that breathing should be co-ordinated with exercise in special ways, but these instructions sometimes merely confuse the exerciser. However, it is a good idea to link breathing out with contraction of the abdominal muscles, therefore the simple command – 'blow out' – will always be inserted with the instructions for abdominal muscle work. Do not worry about 'breathing in' – it happens naturally.

48

THE FIRST FORTY-EIGHT HOURS

BREATHING AND FIRST ABDOMINAL EXERCISE

This exercise improves your circulation, gently tones your abdominal muscles, and helps you to relax.

Lie comfortably on your back with your knees bent, resting your hand on your abdomen. Take a slow deep breath in through your nose, then sigh the air out through your slightly parted lips and draw your abdominal muscles in at the end of the outward breath. Some women are surprised that these muscles should be pulled in at this point, but it is in fact part of the natural breathing pattern. Once you have learnt this sequence, you will then be able to use breathing out to help you relax.

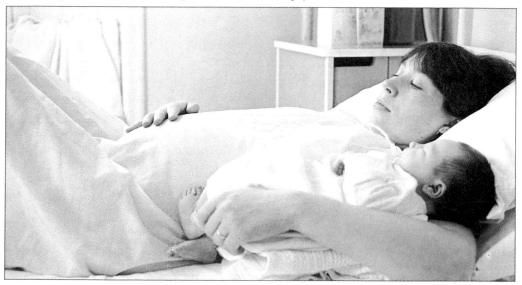

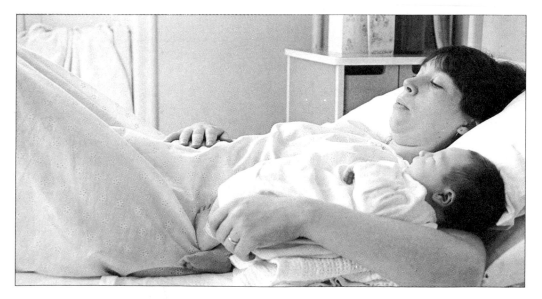

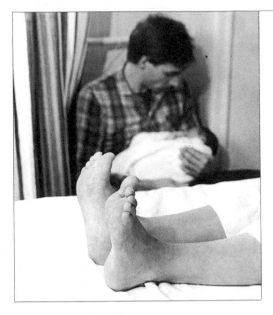

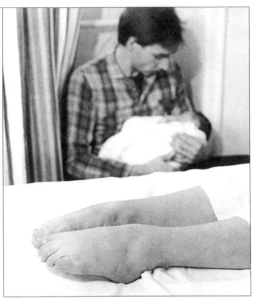

FOOT EXERCISES

These two movements will improve your
leg circulation; they are particularly
important if you are immobilized in bed.

Lie comfortably with your knees
straight and together (above). Bend and
stretch your feet up and down at the
ankles. This should be done briskly and
for about 30 seconds at a time.

Move your feet about 30 cm (12 in)
apart. Then circle your feet twenty times
in each direction (right and below).

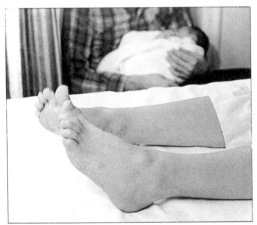

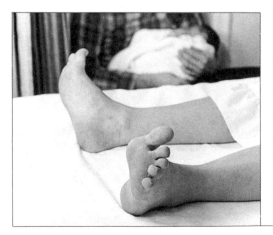

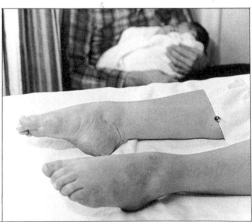

PELVIC ROCKING

This easy exercise has many benefits; it is the basis of good posture and can help ease backache, constipation, and post-Caesarean section abdominal gas.

Lie comfortably with your knees bent and together. Squeeze your buttocks together tilting them upwards. Blow out, drawing in your abdominal muscles and press your back firmly onto the bed. Hold for four counts. When you feel able to, this exercise can be made more difficult by holding the muscle contractions for longer – up to ten counts, and then including the basic pelvic floor exercise with your pelvic rock.

BASIC PELVIC FLOOR EXERCISE

This important exercise strengthens the pelvic floor hammock, and it can help to relieve pain by promoting the reduction of swelling.

Lie comfortably with your knees bent and apart. At first you may be unable to feel your vagina, so start by tightening your anal sphincter. Hold this for four counts, then let it relax. Later, when the sensation is better, imagine that you have a tampon in your vagina that is falling out. Draw your vaginal muscles in and up as if to grip the tampon, hold for four counts, then relax. Try to do this a minimum of four times an hour throughout the day. In the same way that you have to train yourself to become used to a new body posture – bottom and tummy tucked in, ribs well lifted – so you have to become aware of the position of your pelvic floor – your *internal* posture.

You can test your progress by trying to stop or slow down the flow of urine towards the end of your stream. You will gradually regain this control.

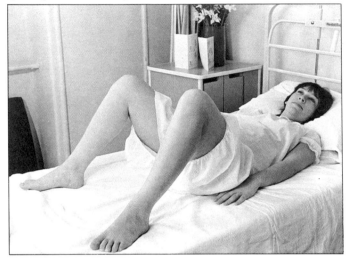

TESTING YOUR ABDOMINAL MUSCLES

If you turn back to page 17 you will see that the two sides of your abdominal girdle nearly always separate towards the end of your pregnancy to accommodate your growing baby. After your baby's birth this gap can be an indication of the strength of the recti abdominis. You cannot feel the separation properly unless you make your muscles work hard. To test yourself, lie on your back with your knees bent up high – pull your abdominal muscles in, lift your head and shoulders and stretch one arm as hard as you can towards your feet. Put the fingers of your other hand just below your umbilicus and feel for the space. Initially almost everyone will have a gap at least two fingers wide – and many people will have a much wider space, three to four fingers wide. As your muscles recover and become stronger, this will gradually close until the gap is so small and tight that you can only insert the tip of one finger.

LEG SLIDING

This is a very efficient tummy toning exercise – it makes both your vertical abdominal muscles (the Recti Abdominis) work very hard, shortening them and helping to close the gap between them.

Lie comfortably on your back with your knees bent and feet flat. Blow out, rocking your pelvis by tightening your abdominal and buttock muscles, so that the back of your waist is pressed very firmly on to the bed. Keeping your back on the bed, slide both feet away from you as far as you can without allowing your back to arch up. Take a breath in, blow out, and, still keeping your back flat on the bed, slowly draw your feet towards your buttocks again.

Initially you may not be able to slide your feet more than a few inches without your back arching, which demonstrates how weak your abdominal muscles are. Gradually your control will improve so that eventually you should be able to straighten and bend your legs completely without losing your back control. Start by doing this exercise four times and gradually increase to twelve.

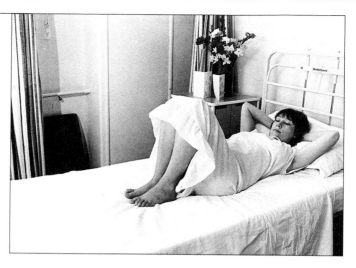

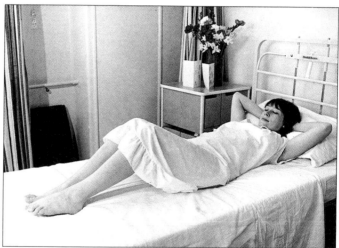

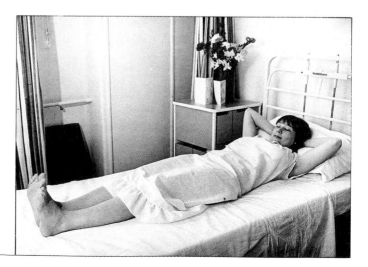

CURL-UPS

This movement strengthens your vertical abdominal muscles.

Lie on your back with your knees bent up high. Blow out and tilt your pelvis up by pulling in your abdominal muscles and drawing your buttocks together while tucking your chin on your chest. Lift your head and shoulders as high as you can, stretching your hands towards your feet. Hold this position for four counts – and then lower slowly. Start with six and increase to twelve.

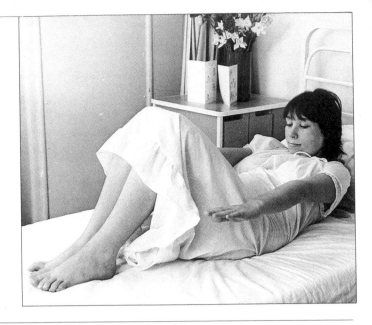

A USEFUL RESTING POSITION AND BUTTOCK TONER

Many women do not realize that once again they can lie flat on their fronts. To do this really comfortably you will need to use two pillows – one under your waist and the other under your head and shoulders. Of course, this position does not flatten or strengthen your abdomen in any way; but after six days have passed it is said to help the uterus to return to its normal position over the bladder. If you have a tender episiotomy, hemorrhoids or backache, you will probably find that rhythmical buttock squeezing while lying on your front, will help relieve your discomfort. Everyone will eventually find this a wonderfully restful position, even those who have had a Caesarean section. It will allow you to relax fully without uncomfortable pressure and could begin toning up flabby buttocks.

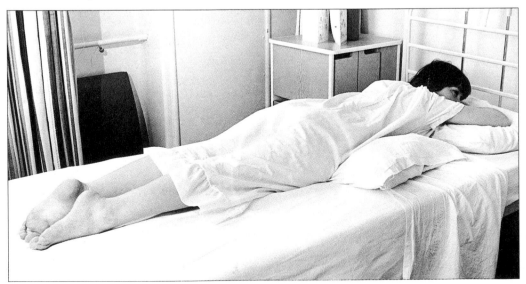

THE POST-CAESAREAN MOTHER

Hints for comfort

If you have had a Caesarean section your needs are somewhat different from mothers who have had normal deliveries, and you will probably receive plenty of help from the nursing staff during your first few days.

You may find your most comfortable position is propped up with pillows, halfway between lying and sitting. A pillow placed under your thighs will prevent you slipping too far down the bed. Make sure that you are really comfortable and well supported for the first few feedings; a pillow across your lap will protect your incision from the weight of your baby. When the time comes for

A pillow placed under your thighs will prevent you from slipping down the bed and another resting across your wound will help prevent too much pain as you feed your baby.

Whichever way you get out of bed, you will find it much more comfortable if you support your Caesarean incision with one or both hands.

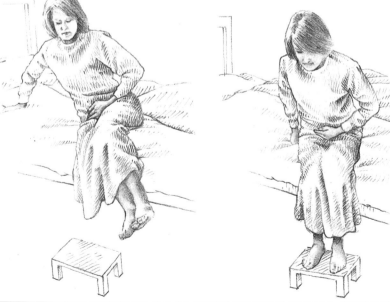

Getting out of bed

you to get up, make sure that your bed is as low as possible. Here are two reasonably comfortable ways to get out of bed:

If you are sitting, edge your bottom towards the side of the bed; then, using your hands behind your thighs, lift your legs out of bed one by one. Brace your abdominal muscles as you straighten up to stand.

If you are lying flat it is easier to roll onto your side, propping yourself first on an elbow; then use both arms to push yourself up so that you are sitting, and then swing your legs over the edge of the bed.

To get back into bed, make sure that you first sit as close to the bed's back support as possible, leaning sideways against the pillows. Brace your abdominal muscles and lift both legs one at a time on to the bed, using your hands to help if necessary. Then, keeping your knees bent and together, roll onto your back.

When you take your first walk to the bathroom you may be tempted to try and protect your sore abdomen by stooping for-wards. You will have less pain however if you can make yourself stand up straight so that the weight of your abdominal organs is off your wound. You may find that gently supporting your wound with your hands will make it easier.

Special exercises

Mothers who have had a Caesarean section can safely do the exercises on pages 49 to 52 as soon as they feel able. They should also do these additional leg and chest exercises.

Leg exercises

These gentle leg movements should be done frequently – ten times, once or twice every hour. They improve your circulation, keep your legs from feeling stiff and help you to feel more relaxed.
1 Sitting comfortably in bed with your legs straight, press your knees down hard onto the mattress, tightening your large thigh muscles. Hold this for four counts and then relax.
2 Draw your buttocks tightly together – hold for four counts, then relax.
3 Bend one leg as high as you can and then slide it down again. Repeat with the other leg.

Breathing and coughing

If you have had a general anaesthetic, you may have extra secretions in your throat and chest. Deep breathing with the emphasis on your outward breath will help to shift these and at the same time will improve your circulation and help you to relax.

If you are "chesty" you may be told to cough, but this will hurt. It will be more comfortable if you lean forwards and support your wound with both hands. Probably the most comfortable position for coughing is sitting on a high chair, leaning forward holding a soft pillow against your abdomen. As normal coughing is too painful, it is best to give a deep "Huff" as you breathe out.

AT HOME

BACK AND BUTTOCK TONER

Lie flat on your front on the floor with your head resting on your hands. Keeping your knees straight, lift your right leg without allowing your pelvis to twist backwards. Hold for four counts and then lower slowly. Do this six times with each leg, increasing to twelve.

Note: Be sure to discuss this particular exercise with a physician before you try it, especially if you have any history of back trouble. Some physicians recommend that you do this standing up to minimize the arching of your back. Support yourself by leaning slightly over a table.

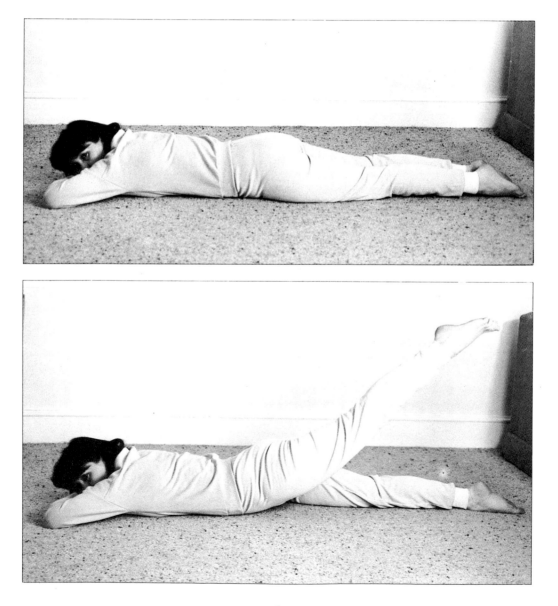

QUICK RELAXATION AND BACK MOBILIZER

This useful exercise can be done almost anywhere and at any time to achieve quick relaxation. It has the added benefit of loosening your tired, tense back muscles.

Sit straight on a chair or stool with your knees and feet wide apart. Curl forward, breathing out so that your arms and head are hanging heavily down. Relax there for a few moments, breathing quietly, feeling the tension draining out of you. Then slowly uncurl your body, straightening your lower back and waist first, followed by your shoulders and finally your head. Hold this relaxed but upright position for a moment, making sure that your shoulders are not hunched up by your ears. Repeat this a few times if you feel the need.

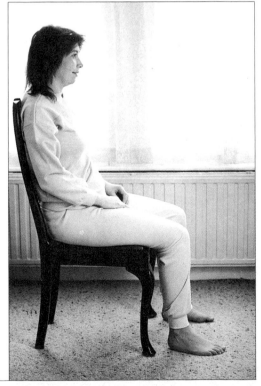

WAIST WHITTLER

With this exercise, you are working the muscles at the sides and front of your waist.

Sit up straight on a chair with your knees and feet apart. Hold your abdomen in firmly and keep your bottom on the chair. Bend sideways to the right, stretching your hand towards the floor. Keeping your tummy flat, straighten up slowly, then relax your abdomen. Repeat the movement to the left.

Be very careful not to allow your body to move forwards or back; the movement should be restricted to a sideways bend, as if your body is fixed between two walls, front and back. Do this four times to each side, increasing to twelve.

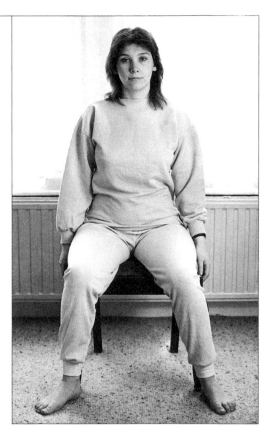

PECTORAL TONER

When you first do this exercise it will probably be helpful to watch yourself in a mirror. You should see a brisk movement of the muscles underlying the breasts, and some women may notice their breasts move too.

Sit up straight on a chair with your knees and feet apart and your arms lifted and bent in front of you; hold your upper arms with the opposite hand. Now push the palms of your hands firmly against your upper arms and stop. You will feel your pectoral muscles con-tracting sharply and then relaxing.

WAIST TWISTER

This exercise uses the diagonal (oblique) muscles of the abdominal corset, firming your tummy and helping to pull in your waist.

Sitting in the same position as for the Pectoral Toner on the previous page, hold your abdomen in hard. Keeping your bottom fixed on the chair and your back erect, twist your body around to the right as far as you can; hold for four counts, then swing around to the left; come back to your starting position and relax your abdominal muscles. Do this six times to each side, increasing to twelve.

DAILY PROGRAM

These sections are designed to help you see at a glance which exercises to do and how many times to do them. Unless otherwise stated, do these sets of exercises *twice a day*. Asterisks mark the most important ones, so when you have very little time you should at least try to fit these in.

The first 48 hours only

BREATHING AND FIRST ABDOMINAL EXERCISE
Circulation, abdominal muscles, relaxation page 49
Do this 4 times every so often

FOOT EXERCISES
Leg circulation page 50
Do the first exercise for 30 seconds, and the second exercise 20 times in each direction, 3 to 4 times a day

The first 48 hours and at home

*PELVIC ROCKING
Posture, backache page 51
6 to 10 rocks, 3 to 4 times a day in the hospital, and twice a day at home

*BASIC PELVIC FLOOR EXERCISE
Pelvic floor muscles page 52
4 times every hour

*LEG SLIDING
Vertical abdominal muscles page 53
4 to 12 times, 3 to 4 times a day in the hospital, and twice a day at home

*CURL-UPS
Vertical abdominal muscles page 54
6 to 12 times, 3 to 4 times a day in the hospital, and twice a day at home

RESTING POSITION AND BUTTOCK TONER
Buttocks, backache page 54
Use the resting position for 15 to 30 minutes.
Squeeze your buttocks 10 times every so often during this rest.

TESTING YOUR ABDOMINAL MUSCLES
page 52
Try doing this test once or twice a week and note the gradual change

POST-CAESAREAN MOTHERS
Remember to do your additional exercises on page 56

At home only

BACK AND BUTTOCK TONER
Buttocks and lower back page 57
6 to 12 times (each leg)

QUICK RELAXATION AND BACK MOBILIZER
Quick relaxation and backache page 58
Do once or twice

WAIST WHITTLER
Side and front waist muscles page 59
4 to 12 times each side

PECTORAL TONER
Pectoral muscles page 60
10 times

WAIST TWISTER
Oblique abdominal muscles page 61
6 to 12 times each side

Post work-out relaxation

Try leaning forwards in your chair (see page 43). Practise your simple relaxation technique (see page 40). Rest like this for as long as possible.

YOUR BABY'S PHYSICAL NEEDS

Having left the enfolding security of the womb for the strange, noisy and vast space of the outside world, your baby will need your warmth and reassurance to help him to adjust to his new environment. Sudden careless movements will startle him and cause him to throw out his arms involuntarily in panic. Babies like calm, confident handling; being wrapped and held securely nearly always soothes and relaxes them. Swaddling is a time-honored way of making a baby feel warm and contented.

Points to consider

In the first six weeks, babies' material needs are few – food, adequate warmth and clothing, and somewhere comfortable to sleep. It is worth remembering this, for you will probably feel rather daunted when you walk into your nearest baby store and see all the paraphernalia that manufacturers seem to believe essential for your child's normal development.

You will probably already have some ideas as to the choice of bed and transport for your baby, based on considerations such as whether you have a car, whether you are going back to work and will be leaving your baby with others, whether you have older children, whether you like to stay at home or walk everywhere, whether you can gladly make do with hand-me-downs or want to have only the newest, best and most fashionable.

You may have taken advice on the safest and best-designed equipment and toys, but there are some important points to consider from your own physical point of view and also for the development of your baby, which you will not be able to learn from the catalogues.

Keeping your baby amused

It is now recognized that a full term newborn baby can see and follow movement with his eyes; he can hear, taste and smell, and within a matter of days has learned to identify the face, voice and smell of his mother. He is, however, completely dependent, and it is only by crying that he is able to convey his needs. His movements are jerky, uncontrolled and often governed by infant reflexes. He is a passive observer, learning through his senses about the world around him.

By about three or four weeks of age he starts to watch his mother intently, following her with his eyes as she moves about, and his own face becomes increasingly alert. He is interested in movement, particularly that of a face, and turns his head towards light, and sometimes to a nearby voice. His body and limbs still remain generally curled up and his hands can only open involuntarily. But by the time he is six weeks old he will enjoy searching his mother's face – especially her eyes and mouth – and will often hold her gaze for several moments, perhaps even breaking into a lopsided smile.

Looking and listening

At this stage a baby does not need toys to play with – he is totally absorbed in learning about his environment, especially the

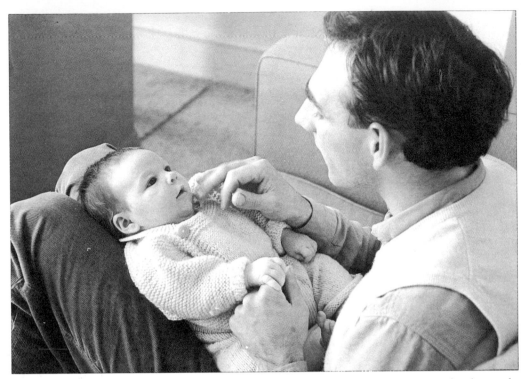

A baby has begun to focus by six to eight weeks. Remember that your face is your baby's most exciting plaything at this age

people most important to him. Of course you can't always be available to him if he lies awake, so you can try taping some large photographs to the side of his crib or a wall hanging nearest where he spends most of his day. A mobile, balloons or a soft toy suspended securely about 20 cm (8 in) above his bed, may provide movement and color to catch his interest and help develop his sensory awareness. A music box playing a soothing tune helps to settle some babies. Remember, however, that you are by far the most exciting thing in your baby's world.

Carrying your baby

Baby carriers are a comforting and natural way to carry babies. They enjoy the warmth, the reassuring sound of a heart-beat and the motion. Being carried in this way is also physically good for them, as it encourages head control and a healthy position of the hips. In Nigeria, where this is the commonest way of transporting babies, congenital dislocation of the hips is hardly ever seen. Carriers are obviously ideal for crowded stores with escalators or walks which are muddy, bumpy or have steps. They are often an answer for the unsettled or colicky baby, who may cease crying and even fall asleep while mother manages a few chores.

Choosing a baby carrier

If you decide to buy a carrier, make sure it has shoulder straps which are well padded and adjustable. If you are short and your partner tall, when either of you wears it you will each need to adjust the supporting straps so that your baby is raised in the pouch as high and near to your respective chins as is comfortable.

This will minimize strain to your backs. Make sure it is not worn to the side, as prolonged carrying of a weight on one side is almost bound to cause backache at this stage.

In their first weeks, babies need firm head support but this will diminish after three or four months and will no longer be necessary by six months, so choose a carrier that can be adjusted accordingly. One of the best carriers has an adjustable inner pouch for the young baby, and an outer pouch for the bigger baby or toddler. A newborn baby nestles in the inner pouch and is almost completely enfolded by the outer one, which acts as head support and extra warmth for the body and limbs. The straps adjust and are well padded, so that it can be used just as successfully to carry a tired toddler on the back as a new baby on the front. The alternatives, which are often cheaper, are sometimes only useful for a brief period of the baby's development – the head support is often no more than an inadequate piece of padding added on to the back support, and the design is often unsuitable to take the weight of a heavier baby with comfort.

If your baby dislikes the carrier

Very occasionally there are babies who do not enjoy carriers and protest as soon as they are put in them. There is also the odd baby who will not tolerate long spells in a carrier and demands to be taken out and allowed to move before being put in again. It is not

Try this secure way of holding your small baby. It will leave you with a free hand while allowing your baby to watch her surroundings as you move about

known why this is so, but obviously it is not worth persevering too long once you have established the carrier to be the cause of his displeasure. If you can possibly try your baby in the carrier of your choice before buying, then it is worth doing so. Most large stores will actually encourage you to do this.

Carrying with one arm

There is another excellent way of carrying your baby without a carrier, but which still leaves one arm free. Using your preferred hand, place your forearm down the front of your baby's trunk with his head resting into the crook of your elbow. His underside arm must be behind your forearm for safety, and your hand can then hold him between the legs. This position stimulates your baby's head control and vision, and you may also find it is an excellent position for bringing up a burp.

Burping your baby

Air bubbles are often mistakenly given as the reason for your baby's crying. While all babies, particularly very young ones, do swallow air as they feed (especially if they are bottlefed), and certainly swallow air if they are left to cry, it is unlikely to be the cause of any incessant crying. Much more likely reasons are hunger, loneliness, overstimulation, feeling hot or cold, fear of loud noises or being dropped, and dislike of being undressed.

You can soothe or burp your baby by holding her over your shoulder so her trunk is elongated, then gently rub her back with your free hand

Positions for
burping

However, if you are in doubt about the reason for your baby's crying after you have fed, changed and cuddled him, it is possible that air trapped in his stomach may be causing temporary discomfort. Put him over your shoulder and very gently pat or rub his back, making sure that you drape him well over the top of your shoulder with his arms hanging down your back. By doing this you are lengthening his trunk so that the burp can escape more readily. If your baby likes to spend a lot of time like this, it is a good idea to try to alternate shoulders, so that you don't get a stiff aching neck on one side.

Another traditional burping position is to hold your baby with one hand open across his chest, and support his head at the chin with your wide open thumb and index finger. Lean your baby slightly forward from the hips while straightening and lengthen-

Even if your baby is breastfed, her father can help by taking over at the end of the feed to burp and change her.

ing his trunk with the supporting hand. At the same time gently rub or pat his back. As your baby may bring back a mouthful of his food with the bubble of air, it is probably a good idea to protect your clothes with a diaper or towel.

Do not continue trying to extract a burp from your baby for too long – five minutes is plenty. Any air that is going to escape from the stomach will do so in this time, so if he continues to cry, try to think of the other possible reasons for his unhappiness.

Three-month colic

If you find that your baby is fretful and tense over a period of a few days at a regular time, particularly the evening, and that in spite of running through all the possible causes of discomfort he is still difficult to pacify for more than a few minutes, you may suspect that colic is the cause. Parents find this distressing

A restless baby can often be soothed in this position. The warmth of a wrapped hot water bottle under her tummy and the comfort of a hand on her back will often send her to sleep at last.

problem very wearing, but babies generally grow out of it by about three months. Discuss it with your pediatrician; in the meantime many parents find that using the following method can soothe a colicky baby quite successfully.

Fill a rubber hot water bottle, and wrap it in a soft towel or diaper. Test that it is not uncomfortably hot; babies can be burned so easily. Lay this lengthwise across your lap and then lie your baby on his front over it. He will probably like to be gently rocked or stroked at the same time.

Sleeping in comfort

A small baby can sleep anywhere that is clean, soft but firm, and draft-free but well-ventilated. A smooth box would do just as well as a fancy crib or carriage. However if you want to be able to move your baby from room to room as he sleeps, or want to take him out in the car, you will need a bed that is portable. As your back is very vulnerable at this point, weight and size should be considered when you make your choice; both a wicker bassinet or a mainly-fabric baby carrier are light and very easy to manage, but as they are not rigid they cannot be safely fastened into a car. If you want a bassinet so that your baby can go in the back of the car, remember that you will be having to lift it onto the seat for the next five to six months. Try and choose a light one that fits in easily without needing any risky twisting movements of your spine and make sure your baby's head is always carried nearest you as you lift the bassinet. Once on the seat it should be secured in place by restrainer straps, part of which may be able to be used to secure a car seat at a later stage.

Baby carriages

Most mothers find a carriage indispensable in the first few months, and some will continue to use it for several years. For many babies it is their first bed; by gently rocking the carriage or taking them out for a walk in it, their parents find they are guaranteed almost certain peace. Parents who also have a young toddler can harness the older child to a special carriage seat, while piling the shopping into the basket underneath. This way the baby is lulled to sleep, the toddler is taken for an outing, and parents bring home all their shopping with no strain to their backs. Of course, the children cannot be left unattended, even for a moment, since the extra weight of a lively toddler can cause even the sturdiest carriage to tilt.

Carriages come in a huge range of sizes, just as they vary from the basic to luxurious. Some separate into a car bed and the frame-and-wheels unit, and still others fold down into strollers. Only you can decide how much and for how long you plan to use a carriage, and can evaluate the importance to you of all the accessories available. Remember that the handle should be at a comfortable height when you push it; also, while having the benefit of accommodating an older sleeping baby, a very large carriage may then be too heavy for you to lift if you need to. Thus your choice of carriage should be based upon considerations not only of your baby and your budget but also of your own various needs and limitations.

Mother and baby medical examinations

Six weeks will be an important milestone for both you and your baby. Your uterus should by now have returned to its pre-pregnancy shape and size, you will probably notice that you have better control of your abdominal muscles and the acute pain from your stitches will have faded. Your baby should by this time be rewarding you with wonderful smiles, have established a fairly regular feeding pattern and have better control of his head. It is for all these reasons that six weeks is generally chosen as the ideal time for a doctor to check both of you.

Your postnatal check-up

This is a very important appointment to keep as it establishes that your body has fully recovered. A blood test may be carried out to see if you are anemic, and your blood pressure will be taken. The obstetrician will want to check that your uterus has fully involuted and he will give you a vaginal examination; he may also want to examine your breasts, whether you are breastfeeding or not, and take a Pap smear for testing if you have not had one within the last year. Now is the time to tell him about any of your postnatal problems, especially if you are finding that intercourse is painful, and to ask his advice. He will ask what you have decided to do about contraception and should discuss this with you.

Your baby's first check-up

Your baby will have been examined thoroughly before being discharged from the hospital, but at four-to-six weeks the pediatrician will give your baby a thorough examination to check his progress. She will record his weight and measure his length and his head and chest circumference. She will look at his eye movements, check his response to sound, and ask you if he has begun to smile. She will also examine his hips and genitals, feel his abdomen and listen to his heart. She will probably check his head control when he is pulled up to sitting. Don't be afraid to mention anything about your baby that is worrying you, however insignificant it may seem.

Six weeks after the birth is a good time to assess the progress of both mother and baby. Not only will you feel physically restored, but your baby's develop-ment will make your relationship much more rewarding

MAKING PROGRESS

EXERCISES
6 WEEKS TO
3 MONTHS

By this time your baby may have have established the beginnings of a routine and will not be so dependent on you for contact if he wakes between feedings. You will have adjusted to the pattern of broken nights and the additional chores and will be able to devote more time and energy to your postnatal recovery.

Your muscles, by no means fully recovered, will have regained some of their strength and you should be ready to move on to stronger, more difficult exercises. In fact, some women will feel ready to tackle this section well before six weeks are up – and there is no reason to hold back if you find that you can cope without undue fatigue or aches and pains. Usually though, and especially if it is your first baby, it does take quite a while to become used to an entirely different life-style, and exercises often have to take second or third place on your list of priorities!

Continue using your feeding times to tone and strengthen your abdominal and pelvic floor muscles. Make sure that you tighten and relax the muscles of the perineum at least twenty times per feeding – still in groups of four – holding each contraction for four counts. Also spend a few moments on your abdominal muscles holding them in for eight to ten counts while continuing to breathe naturally.

You should now try to set aside a short period of time twice a day to concentrate on stronger ways of working these groups of muscles, while adding new exercises for your back, buttocks and legs, plus your chest and arm muscles.

You will probably find by now that your baby is beginning to respond to being moved and handled. He is becoming less passive and will enjoy simple games and activities to help stimulate his development. As he is now more alert and has some head control you can safely put him in a bouncing cradle or lie him near you as you exercise.

Your ligaments are now a little stronger and firmer but have by no means recovered fully. You must still take care when bending, twisting and lifting since they can still be easily damaged.

LYING ON THE FLOOR

PELVIC FLOOR AND STOMACH TRIMMER

This exercise will firm your abdomen, bottom and pelvic floor.

Lie on the floor with your knees bent; if your baby is awake he can sit on your tummy. Draw your pelvic floor muscles inwards and upwards, concentrating on your vagina. Contract your buttocks so that they lift up off the floor; blow out, pulling in your abdomen and lift your head so that your baby can see your face and you can talk to him. Hold this position for four counts, then lower slowly, relaxing all the working muscles. Start with six lifts then progress to twenty. You can also increase the length of time from four to ten counts.

If you still find it difficult to *feel* your pelvic floor working by this stage, it may be helpful after a bath or shower to insert two fingers a couple of inches into your vagina while you stand with one foot on the edge of the bath. Now tighten your pelvic floor muscles. You should feel them gripping your fingers. Constant practice will improve your sensation and power.

THE "UP-CURLER"

This very strong exercise will strengthen your straight abdominal muscles and help to draw them closer together.

Lie on your back with your knees bent up high. Tilt your pelvis up by pulling in your abdominal muscles and drawing your buttocks together at the same time. Tuck your chin onto your chest, blow out and slowly curl your head and shoulders up off the floor, reaching your arms forward to touch your knees. Hold this position for four counts and then lower yourself slowly back to the floor. Do this six times and increase to twenty.

You can increase the length of time you hold the curled-up position from four counts to 30 seconds, and if you cross your arms over your chest when you do your lift, the exercise will be made stronger still.

HIP AND WAIST TRIMMER

This exercise uses your oblique abdominal and lower back muscles to slim your waist.

Lie on the floor with your arms away from your sides and your knees bent up high and feet flat. Pull in your abdominal muscles, then take your knees to the left, until your thigh touches the floor. Keep your knees tightly together and your abdomen firmly in, take your knees to the right and then back to the middle; pause, then repeat. It is important to keep both shoulders flat on the floor as you roll your legs from side to side and *very* important to remember to hold in your abdominal muscles throughout the exercise.

Start with six and increase to twenty, making the exercise more difficult by omitting the pause and increasing the speed of the movement. You may find it helpful to put your hands under your head when you speed up this exercise.

STOMACH FLATTENER AND WAIST SLIMMER

This exercise uses both sets of oblique abdominal muscles.

Lie on the floor, knees bent up high, and your arms by your sides. Pull in your tummy firmly and hold it there. Blow out and stretch your right hand towards your left foot, twisting at the waist. Hold this position for four counts and then lower back again. Repeat with your left hand stretching towards your right foot. You will not be able to reach your foot at first, but gradually you will get closer. Start with six on each side, and increase to twenty.

SIDE-BENDER

This exercise will help flatten your stomach and slim your waist.

Lie on your back with your knees bent up high. Pull your abdomen in firmly and hold it there. Blow out and slide your right hand down towards your right foot, side-bending from your waist. Hold this position for four counts, then, still holding in your abdomen, come back to the starting position. Relax, then repeat to the left. Start with six and increase to twenty.

It is most important to make sure that you continue holding in your abdomen during the movements. This exercise can be made more difficult by omitting the pause between bending to the right and left, and making the movement continuous and faster.

THIGH AND HIP FIRMER

Lie on your right side, resting your head on your right hand with your left hand on the floor in front of you. Pull your abdominal muscles in firmly and hold them there. Lift your left leg straight up sideways as high as you can, without letting it stray forwards or backwards. Hold it there for four counts and then lower. Repeat, lying on your left side. Do this six times each side, increasing to twenty. This exercise can be progressed by holding your leg in the air for longer, up to ten counts.

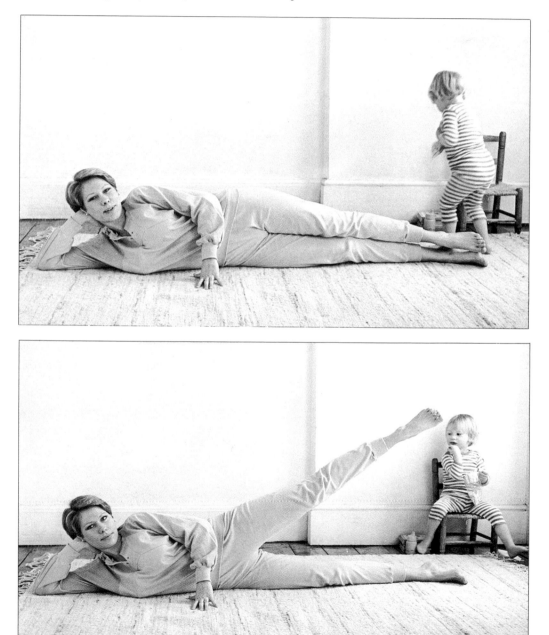

BUTTOCK FIRMER AND BACK STRENGTHENER

Lie on your front and rest your forehead on your hands. Pull your buttocks tightly together then lift both straight legs off the floor. Hold for four counts and lower slowly. Start with six and increase to twenty-four. Remember to breathe normally while your legs are up. If you experience back pain during or after this exercise, leave it out. Note: This particular exercise, and in fact any exercise that requires you to arch your back, should be discussed with a physician before you undertake it, *especially* if you have any history of back trouble.

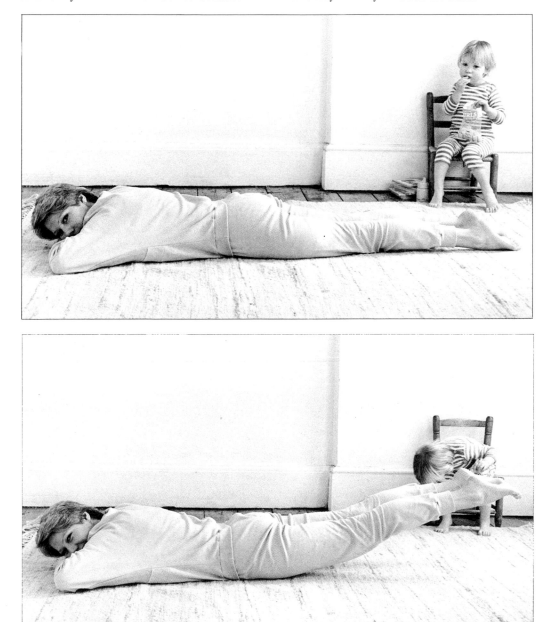

SITTING ON THE FLOOR

THE "DOWN-CURLER"
This works your straight abdominal muscles hard.

Sit up straight with your knees bent and both arms stretched out in front of you. Tilt up your pelvis by holding your abdominal and buttock muscles in firmly. Keeping your back rounded, blow out and curl your body downwards towards the floor. When you reach half way, stop and hold this position for four counts, then slowly return to your starting position. Start with six and increase to twenty.

To make this exercise more difficult, hold the "downcurled" position for up to 30 seconds; continue to breathe normally. Progress further by putting your hands behind your head.

BOTTOM WALKING

This exercise strengthens your back, abdominal and thigh muscles, as well as slimming your waist.

Sit on the floor with your back straight and both legs and arms stretched in front of you. 'Walk' forward on your bottom, keeping your abdominal muscles pulled in tightly at the same time. Take eight 'steps' forwards and eight backwards. Remember to keep your back tall and straight and your abdomen well pulled in as you move. Start with six sequences and increase to twenty. Your baby may enjoy sitting on your lap while you do this exercise.

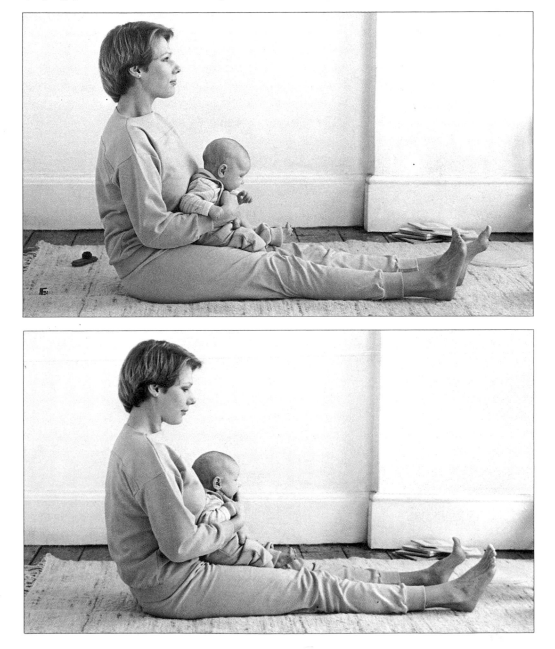

ON ALL FOURS

CAT ARCH

In this exercise you are working your abdominal muscles against gravity. When you are on all fours, you will notice that your tummy really sags when you relax, but when you tighten your muscles to rock your pelvis you can make it quite firm again. This exercise not only strengthens your abdominal muscles but also your buttocks, and it may help to ease an aching back.

Kneel on all fours, with your baby lying on the floor below you so that you can look at one another. Blow out, and arch your back by tightening your abdominal and buttock muscles so that your pubic bone moves forwards. Hold for four counts, then gently relax your muscles so that your back is flat again. Feel the rocking of your pelvis and the muscles that work to do it. Repeat ten times, increasing to twenty.

TAIL-WAGGING

This exercise strengthens the abdominal muscles at your front and sides, helping to firm your waistline.

Kneel on all fours as for the previous exercise, with your baby lying beneath you. Pull in your abdominal muscles to flatten your tummy, then turn your head to the right and bend at the waist so that you can see your right hip. Return to the middle, and now turn your head to the left, bending the waist to move your left hip so you can see it. Repeat ten times, increasing to twenty.

STOMACH AND BACK TONER

This exercise will strengthen the abdominal, back and buttock muscles.

Kneel comfortably on all fours – your baby may enjoy lying on the floor looking up at your face – now try to touch your right knee with your nose and pull your abdomen well in at the same time. Then stretch this leg out and up behind you, feeling your buttocks tighten as you hold the leg in place for four counts. Lower the leg, and repeat the movement on the other side. To start with, try doing this exercise six times on each side and increase it to ten or twelve times.

STANDING UP

THIGH FIRMER

This simple exercise strengthens your postural muscles, firms your buttocks and abdomen and shapes your thighs. Do it gently if you have had knee problems and stop if you experience knee pains.

Hold your baby with his back resting on your chest, your forearm lying across one shoulder and his chest and tummy, with your hand supporting him between his legs. Stand with your back against the wall with your feet slightly apart and about 30-38 cm (12-15 in) from the wall.

Pull in your abdominal muscles and squeeze your buttocks together, tilting your pelvis forward and up. Now, slowly bend your knees and slide 15-30 cm (6-12 in) down the wall, keep your back firmly pressed against the wall from your waist upwards all the time. Hold this position while you count slowly up to six, then gradually straighten your knees again. As you get stronger you can increase the length of time you keep your knees bent – but not so long that the thigh muscles begin to tremble.

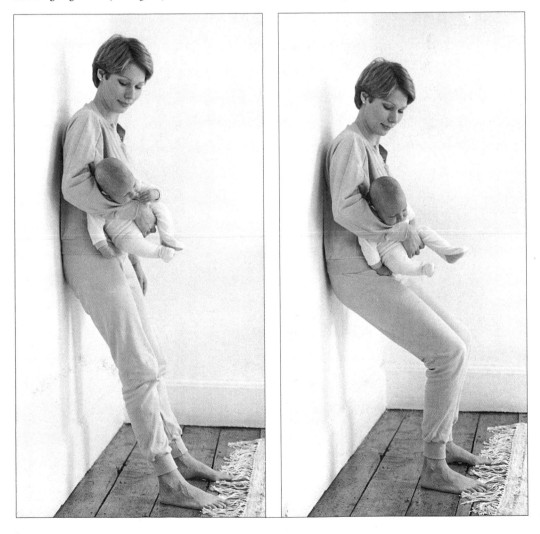

WALL PUSH-UPS

This exercise will strengthen and firm the muscles of your chest and upper arms. It will help you with all the lifting and carrying you will probably be doing by now, but is far less strenuous than regular floor push ups.

Stand with your feet about 60 cm (2 ft) apart. Lean your body weight on your hands, then, keeping your back and legs straight and in line, bend your elbows so that your face is almost touching the wall. Hold for four counts, then straighten your arms and push yourself back. Repeat the exercise ten times at first, gradually increasing it to twenty.

You can work these arm and chest muscles harder by lying face downwards, hands open on the floor just outside your shoulders and pushing your trunk upwards, but, unlike regular floor press-ups, keeping your hips and thighs on the floor. Lower your trunk gently, then repeat slowly, ten times.

DAILY PROGRAM

Reminder Try to do these exercises the recommended number of times, *twice a day*. Asterisks mark the most important exercises so on days when you have very little time at least try to do these.

Lying on the floor

*PELVIC FLOOR AND STOMACH TRIMMER
Abdominal muscles, buttocks, pelvic floor
page 75 6 to 20 times

THE "UP-CURLER"
Vertical abdominal muscles
page 76
6 to 20 times

HIP AND WAIST TRIMMER
Abdominal and lower back muscles page 77
6 to 20 times

*STOMACH FLATTENER AND WAIST SLIMMER
Oblique abdominal muscles
page 78
6 to 20 times

*SIDE-BENDER
Oblique and vertical abdominal muscles
page 79
6 to 20 times

THIGH AND HIP FIRMER
Thighs and abdominal muscles
page 80
6 to 20 times

BUTTOCK FIRMER AND BACK STRENGTHENER
Buttocks and lower back muscles
page 81
6 to 24 times

Sitting on the floor

*THE "DOWN-CURLER"
Vertical abdominal muscles
page 82
6 to 20 times

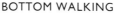

BOTTOM WALKING
Back, abdominal and thigh muscles
page 83
6 to 20 times

On all fours

CAT ARCH
Abdominal muscles, buttocks and backache page 84
10 to 20 times

TAIL WAGGING
Vertical and oblique abdominal muscles
page 85
10 to 20 times

STOMACH AND BACK TONER
Abdominal, back and buttock muscles page 86
6 to 12 times

Standing up

THIGH FIRMER
Back muscles, buttocks, abdominal and thigh muscles
page 87
6 to 20 times

WALL PUSH-UPS
Chest, shoulder and upper arm muscles
page 88
10 to 20 times

Post work-out relaxation

Try lying on your back on the floor (see page 43). Relax like this for at least five minutes.

ENCOURAGING MUSCULAR CONTROL

After six weeks a baby's physical development begins to speed up and there are ways you can help stimulate its natural progress. Exercises for your baby ought to be happy and pleasurable, however; they are not a solemn activity and should be accompanied by talk and cuddles. Never try them when your baby is hungry, tired or unwell, and stop as soon as she starts to cry for any reason. Make sure that she is comfortably dressed and that her clothes do not restrict her activities – ideally she will wear just a diaper and undershirt if the room is warm and the surface soft. A washable pad on the floor may be an ideal surface for the exercises as it is firm, soft and clean.

By about eight weeks your baby will have begun to focus and be interested in watching a moving toy; she can usually follow it from one side to just beyond the midline. At the same time the reflex which kept her hands tightly fisted as a new baby is disappearing and she is generally less curled and floppy. In the next few weeks these open hands and straight, more relaxed arms are going to begin exploring her clothes and bedding. She is still unable to hold a rattle for more than a few moments, and it is not until after she has begun to lie and play with her own hands (about twelve weeks onwards) that she will understand the vital relationship between eyes and hands and begin to reach for what she wants. She shows her excitement at seeing a bright toy held in front of her by kicking and waving her arms furiously and she may hit it by chance but is still unable to explore it.

Helping your baby to play

Although she has not yet learned to grasp an object she is full of yearning to do so. Choose objects that are reasonably large, lightweight and bright, and make a noise when banged, and hang one or two of them over her crib or bouncing cradle (see page 95); she will swipe at them with her arms and occasionally make contact, perhaps producing a noise which draws her attention to what her hands are doing. A large fluffy ball with a bell inside, brightly colored teething rings, or an aluminum foil plate can be just as absorbing as an expensive commercial cradle game for this purpose. Once you have engineered the hanging device, perhaps with just a piece of elastic, you can use your ingenuity to think of exciting changes. As long as they are light, have no sharp edges and are fastened securely, then you have an almost endless supply in your own home.

Improving visual control

To improve your baby's visual control, catch his attention so he follows your face with his eyes

By about twelve to sixteen weeks a baby begins to turn her head towards the source of a sound; and she can follow a moving object with her eyes from one side over to the other. You can make a game of this activity to help stimulate these vital head and visual movements.

Lie your baby on her back and dangle a bright rattle above her, about 20-30 cm (8-12 in) away, to catch her attention. Slowly move it in an arc, waiting for her eyes and head to follow – rattle it

to revive her interest if she loses it. Try moving the rattle back to the midline, and beyond it towards the opposite side as well.

Some babies may cooperate in this game far better if it is a familiar face they are required to follow. Try moving your face from the middle to one side, back to the middle and over to the opposite side, talking all the time to keep your baby's attention.

Developing head control

By about two months your baby will be beginning to use her neck muscles to control her head when she is pulled to sitting. You can help her develop this important ability by practicing it gently with her when she is seated on your lap.

Strengthening front neck muscles

Sit comfortably with your feet raised on a footstool. Lie your baby lengthwise along your thighs, meanwhile talking to her. Put your thumbs into her palms and wrap your fingers around the back of her hands, turning her palms towards one another. Now straighten her elbows and start to lift her head and body gently towards you, talking to her as you do so. Wait a moment and you will see her head begin to lift in line with her shoulders. Pull her slowly up towards you as far as she can manage while keeping her head controlled and in line with her body, and then lower her gently back. This strengthens her neck muscles and helps her learn to control her head in preparation for sitting.

You can develop your baby's head control by lying him along your thighs and lifting him slowly towards you while you talk to him

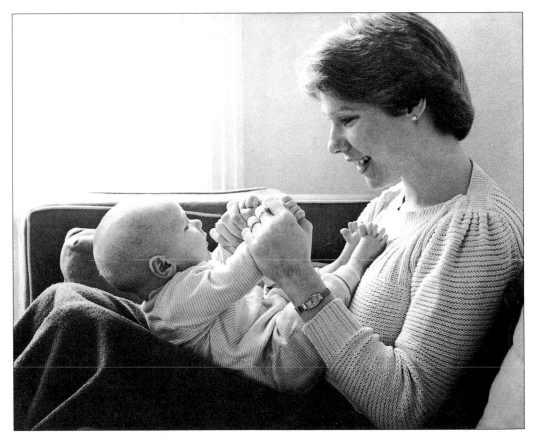

Babies love to be handled, and tipping your baby gently to one side (making sure his head is always in line with his body) makes a delightful game. Do not tilt so far that his head drops down

Strengthening side neck muscles

Another way to stimulate her head control is by tilting her sideways, allowing her time to keep her head in line with her body. Stand with your feet comfortably apart, holding your baby under her arms as you tilt her. Your head and shoulders will tilt also and you can talk to her as she holds this position for a few moments; then slowly return to the middle and tilt her the other way.

By about three months her neck muscles should be able to keep her head steady when she is tilted from side to side. Doing this gently as an exercise will help strengthen these muscles, and it can be repeated several times a day.

Strengthening your baby's back

By now your baby is probably needing less sleep during the day, and is no longer happy to be put straight back to bed after

It is important for all babies to spend some time lying on their fronts. Placing a rolled towel under your baby's shoulders helps to strengthen his back, while an elder brother or sister may enjoy being involved as well to attract the baby's attention

every feeding. When you hold her you will notice she is beginning to look about and that she is getting stronger and can lift her chin off the mattress when lying on her stomach.

Help to strengthen your baby's back with the following exercise. Roll up a clean towel to about eight thicknesses – about 6 cm (2½ in) diameter – and place it on the floor. Gently lower your baby onto her front so that her forearms rest on the floor and the towel is under her chest. Now talk to her or use a toy to attract her attention so that she lifts her head up. She will begin to work the muscles of her neck and back – some of the muscles she needs to strengthen for sitting – and learn to take weight through her forearms. You may find that gently rubbing or pressing her spine will help stimulate her to lift her head and straighten her back. Repeat this activity several times a day for as long as your baby is happy. If your baby is not used to lying on her front and cries when first put in this position, then see if you can distract or soothe her for a few minutes before lifting her up, and try the position again a little later.

Strengthening neck and shoulders

While you are enjoying socializing with your baby, you can also be encouraging her to strengthen the muscles of her neck and shoulders. Lie comfortably on a sofa with your head propped on an armrest and your baby on your chest. Bring her elbows forward

While they enjoy each other's smiles, in this rewarding game father can relax while his baby strengthens his neck, arms and back

Using a bouncing cradle

and in so that they lie beneath her shoulders and she can support some weight through her forearms. Talk to her so that she wants to lift her head to look at you and, as she does so, you will feel her pressing down through her elbows and forearms and you can accordingly lessen your support. Repeat this wonderfully friendly activity as often and for as long as you both enjoy it.

Now is the time you may decide to buy your baby her first "chair", a bouncing cradle, made of fabric or firm plastic on a cantilevered metal frame. She is well supported in a bouncing cradle and is tilted slightly upwards so that she can watch you while you are busy. You can suspend things of interest in front of her or fix one of the specially designed toys to the frame of the cradle. This type of chair is safe until the baby has started to lift up her head and shoulders, which may be at about five months. While she plays in it, the increasing movements of her arms and legs will gently rock the frame, and that in itself usually delights her even more. It is also light and portable enough for you to take about the house as you move from room to room, but remember that even the smallest rocking motions are enough to move the chair, and it is *never* safe placed unfixed on a table or kitchen worktop.

FIT FOR LIFE

EXERCISES
3 TO 6 MONTHS

If you have been able to do your exercises with some regularity and enthusiasm, your muscles will now be much stronger and firmer and your body will look and feel much better than it did. Even if your baby hasn't allowed you time for yourself and you have been unable to do any but the most basic exercises, you will still notice that your shape has begun to return.

The exercises in this section are very much stronger and will therefore do much more for your figure. If you feel confident about the strength of your muscles, it is perfectly safe to follow the program exactly. However, if you are uncertain, start slowly and gently – keeping the repetitions to a minimum until you are sure that you are not straining yourself. The test given on page 52 to find your diastasis recti (the gap between the vertical abdominal muscles) will tell you what progress you have made. By now you should find that the gap has nearly closed and that your muscles feel much firmer. Opposite you will find a strenuous test for that other group of important muscles – the pelvic floor.

Your baby by now will be quite delightful and thoroughly rewarding. Apart from allowing him to join you in your exercises you will want to use your playtimes with him to help his physical progress in every way. He is rapidly learning to control his head, limbs and body and you will find that very soon he will be rolling and sitting. He will already be communicating his needs and pleasures very clearly and using his voice in various ways. Exercising with him now should be great fun for you both.

Soon you will want to move on from the restricting, and sometimes solitary routine of postnatal exercises and will be wondering when it is safe to resume normal sport. Obviously this will depend enormously on how fit you were just before your baby's birth, and the type of sport you are planning to take up. In the section "Resuming Normal Exercise" (page 124) there is some basic advice on your choices and the activities best avoided. By the time your baby is six months old you should certainly feel "Fit for Life!"

PELVIC FLOOR CONTROL

THE ULTIMATE TEST

By the time your baby is six months old you should no longer have any discomfort from your stitches and the strength of your pelvic floor muscles should be back to normal, so that you can control your bladder when you cough, sneeze, or pick up your baby.

The ultimate test for your pelvic floor control is to jump up and down in place, eventually trying with your legs apart, coughing at the same time – your panties should stay dry. This does not mean that you can forget your pelvic floor exercises until you have your next baby. Ideally every woman should be aware at all times of this hammock of muscles and the role it plays in her day to day activities and sex life, so continue tightening and relaxing these muscles a few times a day for the rest of your life.

SQUAT TIGHTENING

Squat down, preferably with your heels flat on the floor, holding on to a chair if you find it difficult to balance yourself. If you can't squat with your heels down comfortably try it with shoes on (a small heel sometimes makes all the difference). Your pelvic floor muscles have to work harder in this position than when you are sitting, standing or lying.

Tighten the ring of muscles around try to feel the contraction of the muscles around your urethra too. Hold the muscles tight while you count to four and then relax. Repeat twelve times in groups of four. If you find this tiring, do four, rest, and then do another four. Do this exercise three to four times a day.

LYING ON THE FLOOR

PELVIC LIFT

This exercise is good for your pelvic floor, buttock and back muscles.

Lie on the floor with your heels resting on a low chair; your baby can lie or sit on your tummy. Tighten your pelvic floor muscles, lifting inwards and upwards; at the same time draw your buttocks tightly together and raise them off the floor so that your body is in a straight line from heels to your head. Hold this position for four counts and then lower. Do it six times and increase to twelve. This exercise can be progressed by holding your buttocks in the air for longer – up to ten counts.

CYCLING

This exercise is good for your leg and abdominal muscles.

Lie on your back with your knees bent up to your chest. Blow out and lift your head from the floor. Keeping your left knee pulled up close to you, stretch the right leg out until it is straight and about 15 cm (6 in) from the floor. With a cycling motion, change legs so that your left leg is then stretched out. Repeat for six sequences then lower your knees and relax. Progress to twenty sequences.

It is vitally important that you brace your abdominal muscles and make sure that the back of your waist is pressed down firmly on the floor throughout the movement. If your back is arching up as you 'cycle' your legs, it indicates that you are not yet ready for this strong exercise. Concentrate on the less strenuous ones for a while longer.

KNEE ROLLING

This exercise slims the waist and hips.

Lie on your back with your hands behind your head and your legs straight. Holding your knees and feet together, blow out, pull in your tummy, and bend your knees up tightly on to your chest. Keeping your abdominal muscles pulled well in, let your knees roll slowly to the right until your thigh touches the floor. Rest for a moment; then, bracing your abdominal muscles once again, bring your knees up to the middle. Repeat to the left. Do this sequence six times and increase to twenty-four.

This exercise can be made more difficult by taking the knees over from side to side without pausing in the middle, and also by increasing the speed of the movement.

SCISSORS

This exercise tones, shapes, and strengthens your thighs and also your abdominal muscles.

Lie on your back with your legs straight. Blow out, rock your pubic bone upwards and bend both legs together on to your chest, keeping your back pressed onto the floor. If you are unable to do this yet, slide both feet up to your buttocks and then bend your knees up on to your chest. Now stretch your legs up so that they are at a right angle to your body. Make sure that you keep your back firmly pressed on to the floor throughout this movement. Pulling your abdomen in all the time, open and close your legs, stretching them as wide apart as you can and crossing them first one way and then the other in the middle, like scissors.

Do this eight times, then bend your knees on to your chest and stretch your legs back on to the floor, still keeping your back pressed down hard. Slide your feet down if your back cannot yet take the strain of the final stretch. Do this sequence four times to start with, progressing to twelve.

WAIST, HIP AND THIGH TRIMMER

This exercise strengthens abdominal and thigh muscles, and helps to trim a thick waist.

Lie on your side, resting your head on your hand, and balancing yourself with your other hand in front of your body.

Brace your abdomen and buttocks. Blow out, and lift both legs up sideways; hold for four counts and then lower slowly. Do this six times and then turn onto your other side and repeat. Start with six leg lifts; then progress by increasing to twelve each side.

SITTING ON THE FLOOR

FULL SIT-UPS

This exercise will continue strengthening and tightening your straight abdominal muscles, returning them to full normality.

Sit with your knees bent up high and both arms stretched out in front of you. Blow out, pull in your abdominal muscles and tuck your buttocks under; then slowly curl downwards allowing your back to reach the floor, vertebra by vertebra. Relax. Blow out and pull your abdominal muscles in again, then curl upwards so that you are sitting up straight once more. This exercise can be made more difficult by omitting the relaxing pause when you reach the floor and then by putting your hands behind your head.

Only begin this very strong exercise when you feel you can really control the movement without collapsing back onto the floor or having to jerk yourself up to begin the up-curl. Start with four and progress to sixteen.

KNEELING EXERCISES

KNEELING TWISTS

This firms your thighs, buttocks, waist and pelvic floor.

Kneel up straight on the floor with your arms crossed and lifted in front of you. Remembering to keep your abdominal and buttock muscles firmly pulled in, sit yourself on the floor on your right. Now lift up, holding abdomen and buttocks firmly and adding a pelvic floor "lift" at the same time, then change to sitting on your left.

Keep the movement controlled, and don't bump your buttocks down too hard on the floor – you will not be working the muscles effectively and you may bruise yourself. Start with eight, then progress to sixteen and finally to twenty-four.

LEANBACKS
This exercise will firm your thighs, buttocks, abdominal muscles and pelvic floor.

Kneel up straight with both arms stretched out in front of you. Tuck your buttocks under, your stomach in, and lift your pelvic floor up, blow out and lean back slowly as far as you can. Hold the position for four counts and then return to your starting position. Start with six lean backs and increase to twenty. You can make this exercise harder by holding your baby in your arms in front of you. Do it in front of a mirror so that your baby will be amused to see you both come and go as you lean back and straighten up (see pages 117-8).

THE FINAL TEST

ELBOW TO KNEE TWISTS

This exercise makes all your abdominal muscles work very powerfully, testing the work you have been putting in to them.

Lie on your back with both knees bent up high and your hands behind your head. Pull in your abdominal muscles firmly, blow out and tuck your chin onto your chest, bringing your left elbow to touch your right knee. Hold for four counts and lower slowly. Repeat to the other side using the opposite elbow and knee. This exercise can be made tougher by holding the elbow-to-knee position for longer, and then by keeping both feet flat on the floor as you come up.

AT THE SWIMMING POOL

WAIST TWISTER

This exercise works the vertical abdominal muscles as you draw your knees to your chest and the diagonal (oblique) abdominal muscles as you twist, trimming your waist.

Stand with your back to the sides of the pool, stretching your arms out along the rail. Pull in your abdominal muscles, and draw your knees up to your chest. Hold the position, keeping your knees pressed together and your abdominal muscles tight, while you twist your knees to the right side as far as you can. Hold while you count to four, return to the middle, and repeat the twisting movement to the left. Now return to the middle and relax. Repeat this complete sequence ten times, increasing to twenty.

WATER CURL-UPS

This exercise will require your vertical abdominal muscles to work hard against the water's resistance. You will also work your back and buttock muscles to regain and maintain your floating position.

Face the rail at the deep end and hold it with your arms bent and your legs stretched out behind you, so that you are floating. Pull in your abdominal muscles, grip your legs together, and slowly bend your knees up towards your chest. Hold to the count of four, then relax your legs so that they drop down. Now gently kick your legs so that they are once again floating out behind you, and repeat the exercise. Start with ten and increase to twenty times.

WAIST SWING

In this exercise, you are working the muscles at the front and sides of your waist against resistance, hence firming and strengthening them. At the deep end, hold on to the rail with your back to the side of the pool. Let yourself relax with your legs straight and together, then pull in your abdominal muscles and gently swing your body and legs from the waist down – first to the left, keeping your shoulders and upper trunk still, and then to the right. Repeat ten times to each side, increasing to twenty.

DAILY PROGRAM

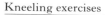

Reminder Try to do these exercises the recommended number of times, *twice a day*. Asterisks mark the most important exercises, so on days when you have very little time at least try to do these.

Pelvic floor control

*SQUAT TIGHTENING
Pelvic floor muscles
page 99
12 times

Lying on the floor

PELVIC LIFT
Pelvic floor, buttock and back muscles page 100
6 to 20 times

CYCLING
Leg and abdominal muscles
page 101
6 to 20 times

KNEE ROLLING
Oblique abdominal and lower back muscles
page 102
6 to 20 times

SCISSORS
Thighs and abdominal muscles page 103
4 to 12 times

*WAIST, HIP AND THIGH TRIMMER
Abdominal and thigh muscles
page 105
4 to 12 times

Sitting on the floor

*FULL SIT-UPS
Vertical abdominal muscles page 105
4 to 20 times

Kneeling exercises

KNEELING TWISTS
Thighs, buttocks, abdominal muscles and pelvic floor muscles page 106
8 to 20 times

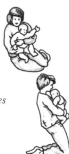

LEANBACKS
Thighs, buttocks, abdominal muscles and pelvic floor muscles page 107
6 to 20 times

At the swimming pool

WAIST TWISTER
Vertical and oblique abdominal muscles page 109
10 to 20 times

WATER CURL-UPS
Vertical abdominal muscles, back and buttock muscles
page 110
10 to 20 times

WAIST SWING
Vertical and oblique abdominal muscles page 111
10 to 12 times

The final tests

When you can do both these exercises you're ready for anything

*ELBOW TO KNEE TWISTS
All abdominal muscles page 108
6 to 20 times

THE ULTIMATE PELVIC FLOOR TEST
Pelvic floor muscles page 99
Do once after the first 3 months and occasionally thereafter

Post work-out relaxation

Try lying on your back in the yoga "corpse" position (see page 43). Relax like this for at least five minutes.

LEARNING THROUGH PLAY

For babies, the age of three to six months is an intense period of socializing – they are obviously beginning to understand their surroundings, and are just as capable of excitement at the sight of people or toys they like as they are of anger at being denied something they want. Their heads can now move independently but they do not have full control until about five to six months. Although by four months babies can hold their heads up well while sitting, when they are pulled from a lying position their heads still lag behind at the beginning of the movement.

Helping head control

You can help strengthen your baby's neck muscles by practicing this exercise every time you pick him up from lying, provided he is not tired or unhappy. Lie your baby on the carpet and kneel down facing him, with one of your knees positioned between his legs. Move your face closely towards him and catch his attention by talking to him. Put your thumbs in his palms and wrap your fingers around his hands, then gently pull his arms straight and begin to lift him upwards. Wait for him to co-operate and work his neck, arm and tummy muscles – you will see his head begin to pull into line with his body and feel his arm and tummy muscles helping you pull him up. Reward him with a smile or a cuddle each time he does it.

Propped sitting

Another way of helping develop head control is to prop your baby in a sitting position. By three to four months babies can hold their heads up well enough to enjoy sitting and looking around,

Once your baby is three months old, with supervision an older child – like this baby's sister – can help to develop your baby's vital head control in preparation for sitting

Right : As early as three to four months, you can prop your baby in a carriage, lessening the support as her strength and control improve. Even at this age, however, make sure your baby wears a safety harness Opposite : Rolling is your baby's first step to mobility. Start by attracting her attention to one side (top), then encourage her to turn by easing her leg over (below), making sure she does most of the work

their backs being fairly straight, though not yet in the lower part. By five months their heads are even more stable and spines still straighter, and they almost demand to be sat up to watch and play. If you have a carriage it is the ideal place to teach your baby the early skills needed for sitting. Use small cushions or folded blankets to prop behind and to the sides as necessary, and a rolled blanket under his thighs if his bottom slips forward. As his sitting improves, move him further upright and lessen his support, but always harness even a young baby for safety. Loosely suspend some rattles on elastic across the carriage so that he can swipe at or reach for them, but make sure that if he slides down the carriage the elastic will not harm him.

Learning to roll

While your baby is learning how to remain erect in preparation for sitting, he is also beginning to learn to twist or rotate his trunk so that he can roll. This movement of the body is necessary for crawling and later walking, when the leg of one side will move with the arm of the other. By about five to six months most babies will have learned to roll from their fronts onto their backs, and by about a month later will be able to roll the other way. You can show your baby how to roll from an early age when you are changing his diaper – only be careful that you never leave him unattended on a high surface in case he decides he can do it by himself.

Start with your baby on his back, lying on an unrestricted, firm, but comfortable area, for instance a clean carpet or a blanket on the floor. With your left hand, attract his attention with a bright, noisy rattle about 30 cm (12 in) to the right of his face so that he turns to look at it. Now put your right hand behind his left knee, bending it up and pressing the back of your outstretched fingers onto his right thigh to keep it flat. Roll his left hip forward and over towards the right side, waiting for him to follow with his

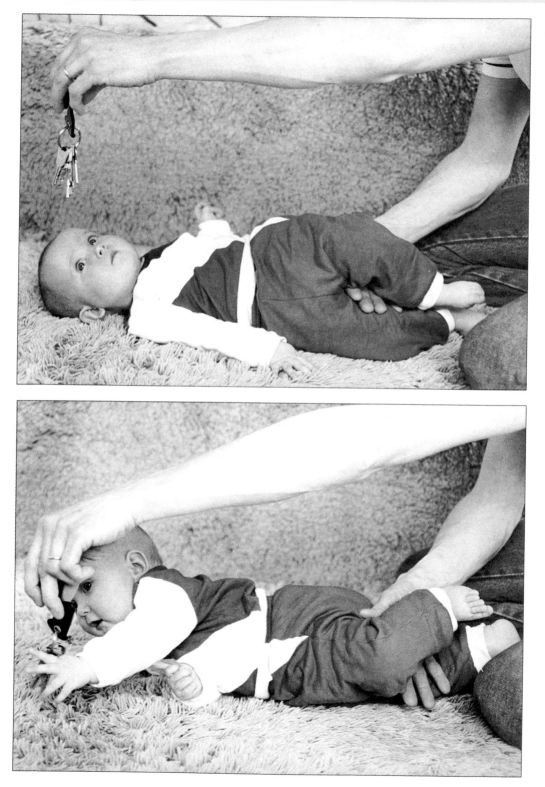

Once your baby discovers her feet, help her gain strength and control of her legs by dangling toys where she can reach them with her toes

upper trunk and shoulders. When you reverse the movement, tuck the right arm under his chest so that his left shoulder naturally falls backwards. Be careful that you are ready to support his head if he needs it, as the movement in this direction is often effortless and rather speedy. Don't forget to roll him in the other direction too. This movement will quickly become natural, and you will be able to decrease your assistance as he learns to rotate his body himself – leading either with an arm or a leg.

Encouraging foot play

At about five months or perhaps a little later, babies have usually begun to learn about their feet by feeling and holding them with their hands, and using them to hit at toys the way they have already have learned to do with their hands. This is an important stage of their development as it teaches them body awareness and how to begin controlling their legs.

You can help to develop this skill through play. Try holding your baby's hands while suspending a mobile or 'cradle gym' above his hips, so that he can easily see it. You may need to arouse his interest first by touching his foot against it and making it move or rattle. Now wait and see if he moves his own feet back up to it to play with it himself. He will probably enjoy this activity best if he is lying without a diaper on.

Back and arm strengtheners

By about five months babies have enough strength in their backs and arms to take weight on their hands when they lie on their fronts – their straight arms lifting their chests and upper abdomens off the floor.

You can exercise and further strengthen these important muscles by encouraging your baby first to look at a toy dangled in front of his face and then above his head, and finally to reach for one, all while he is lying on his front. To start with he will probably only be able to take weight on one straight arm for a brief moment, and reach for a toy on or only just above the ground. As his strength and coordination improve you will be

Right: The mirror game helps to strengthen your baby's back and neck muscles while amusing her with one of the most fascinating people in her life – herself! Make sure the chest support is as little as necessary, to allow her back muscles to work hard

Below: Encourage your baby to push up with straight arms by attracting her attention above her head

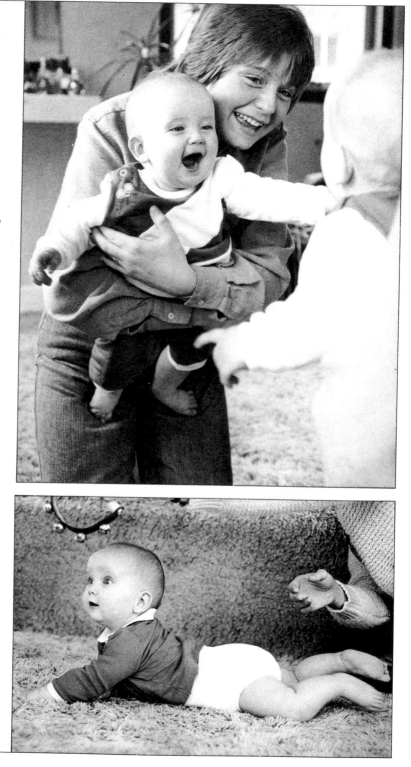

Neck and back strengthener

able to hold the toy further up in the air so that he has to reach for it – but never allow him to become frustrated and upset by this game. It should be fun for you both.

You can further strengthen your baby's neck and back muscles by playing with him in front of a mirror. Kneel down holding your baby with his back to you, facing a large mirror. By about five months he will probably like to smile at his own reflection, so give him time to see himself in the mirror before you start. With his feet on your thighs (he will probably enjoy standing on you at this stage), hold one hand in front of his knees and the other supporting his chest, and slowly lower him towards the mirror. Allow his head and back to work as you lower him, giving him minimal support under his chest. He may begin to talk to himself in the mirror. Hold him there as long as he is happy and you are comfortable.

Encouraging your baby to sit

With the increased strength of his back muscles and his strong neck muscles, your baby is now almost ready to sit alone.

When he has begun to learn how to balance, you can try sitting him on the floor between your legs, with a few inches separating his body from your legs. If he still relies on his arms to prop him up in front, try offering him a toy so that he will reach out with one arm. Gradually he will learn to extend his spine even further and sit up without the help of his arms.

When your baby is almost sitting, play with her on the floor sometimes so that your legs act as cushions. Once she is able to balance without propping on her arms you can encourage her to reach to either side for a toy

Sitting but not yet safe

By about five to six months your baby will possibly be able to sit up without leaning on his arms, but he will probably not yet have learned the final balance and protective reactions which make sitting alone a stable and safe position. A large cardboard box is the ideal place to put him at this stage; sit him in one corner where the soft sides prevent him falling, and surround him with his favorite toys so he feels safe and secure.

Sitting balance

Once your baby can sit on your knees without support, you can develop his sitting balance further while playing a game. Perhaps to the words of nursery rhymes, like *Rock-a-Bye Baby* or *Twinkle, Twinkle, Little Star,* you can lift one leg and then the other, starting with small, regular movements, and progressing to larger, less predictable movements, always having your hands free and ready to catch him if he is tipped off balance.

The parachute reaction

From about six months, babies learn to 'save' themselves when pushed forwards while sitting or when lowered head first towards the ground: they react by straightening their arms and putting out their hands to protect their heads. This vital activity is called the parachute reaction and can first be learned and later reinforced in play. If you hold your baby at his trunk and lower him, at first very gently, towards a soft surface such as a bed, he will soon learn to put his arms out, meanwhile straightening his back and lifting his head. This reaction will be particularly important for his early days of walking when he will fall frequently.

For safety without too much support, let your baby sit and play in a sturdy cardboard box, surrounded by toys

**Bath-time
swimming**

Once your baby begins to enjoy his bath, you may like to allow him an occasional "swimming lesson". Run a deep bath and, if you prefer, put inflated armbands on his upper arms before lowering him into it. Let him kick and splash a little, enjoying the water lapping around his face, and teach him to start blowing bubbles in the water. Make sure you don't leave him for a second, for obviously he has no sense of self-preservation. It is, and should be, a great game to him, and while he is enjoying himself, he is developing neck and back muscles but above all, gaining confidence in the water.

Taking your baby
to the swimming
pool

After these first "swimming lessons" in the bath, you can try taking him to a real swimming pool. Once he has completed his first set of immunizations he will be safe to go in the water, provided he is well and the water and air around it warm.

The best way to start is to take your baby into the shallowest part of the pool and just hold him securely, letting him feel the water and absorb his surroundings. Once he is confident, you gently lower him into the pool on his back, supporting him with one open palm under his center of gravity (probably about waist level), while keeping your other forearm and hand under (but not supporting) his neck and head, in case he tips back. Now let him feel the water lapping around his face and body, and enjoy the random movements of his limbs.

*Above : Bathtime can
be the start of
swimming lessons. With
one hand supporting
her waist, let her kick,
splash and blow
bubbles. Your free
hand is ready to
protect her face from
accidental immersion*

Once he has good head control at about five or six months, you can start turning him onto his tummy and supporting him under the chest. He will kick and splash – but watch that he doesn't inhale large amounts of water when he joyfully dips his head under.

Play and toys

At about three months babies discover their own hands; a few weeks later they learn how to bring them together, to feel objects with them, and to play with rattles which are placed in their hands. By five months they have learned the vital combination of reaching for and getting something they see and want, and they then manipulate it, chew it, bang it and transfer it from hand to hand. By about six months they are sometimes beginning to reach with one hand, and to examine objects very closely on all sides by turning their wrists over.

The toys they need at this stage are few and simple. The first rattle should be one that is bright and attractive, light, well-balanced and easy to hold in a small fist. It should be safe and pleasurable for biting and mouthing, and make a pleasant noise when moved or shaken. The dumb-bell rattle is an ideal choice, as are teething rings. A squeaky, ridged plastic clutch ball, an unbreakable, plastic-rimmed mirror, and some coloured wooden blocks are guaranteed to give hours of pleasure. "Cradle gyms" suspended across the crib or carriage, and activity boards attached to the rails of the crib are worth investing in to amuse your baby. Small soft toys are now worth introducing as they are ideal for this period when the face gets a lot of banging, and they are easy to manipulate in one hand. Babies are wonderfully responsive playmates at this stage, but although you will be finding every new development fascinating, you will probably also be pleased to see how much better your baby is able to occupy himself for a few minutes with his favorite toys, a zwieback or just a wooden spoon or some paper to crumple. It is really unnecessary to spend a lot of money on toys for a baby of this age.

Baby walkers and bouncers

Although many babies of five to six months enjoy spending time in baby walkers or bouncers, they should not be left in either of these for long periods of the day. The standing ('extensor') phase is only transient and prolonged use of a walker or bouncer can actually inhibit the natural progression beyond it. Babies need to learn to roll, rotate their bodies and move one part or side separately from another as well as simply straightening and pushing with their legs.

Bouncers can cause babies to develop abnormally persistent stiffness of their legs if they remain suspended in them for long periods. At the most, fifteen to twenty minutes in a bouncer at any one time is probably all right, provided the baby has plenty of other opportunities to move freely in other positions.

Cribs for the older baby

By now your baby will probably be rapidly outgrowing her first bed and you will be ready to move her into a full-size crib. Modern portable cribs may be worth consideration as they are safe, sturdy, collapsible and often cheaper than ordinary cribs. However, if you have a back problem, then the conventional drop-side crib will obviously make lifting your baby out much easier and more comfortable. When choosing a drop-side crib, make sure the movable side has a childproof mechanism for releasing it, and that the bars are no more than 6 cm ($2\frac{1}{2}$ in) apart.

Transporting the older baby

Strollers

Safety car seats

As your baby approaches six months, you will find he appreciates outings more, and your own movements will be far less restricted or complicated.

The collapsible stroller is now an almost vital addition to your baby equipment – it is so much lighter and more compact than a carriage. At about three to four months a normal baby may be safely tried in a reclining stroller. If he gradually slips to one side you may be able to make adjustments with a rolled blanket so that he is snugly supported.

Try a short excursion at first to see how he copes with his new transport. Babies do not suffer in silence, so if he is alert and happy, then it is doing him no harm. He will probably not be able to cope with a stroller in the erect position until he is five to seven months, as he will not have developed the balance reactions in his trunk to keep him upright until then. Remember to choose a stroller which has handles at a comfortable height for you as you will probably have many hours of pushing ahead.

Babies usually have full head control between five and a half and six and a half months; if their bodies are moved they can keep their heads in line and hold them steady. It is now safe to put your baby in a car seat, provided the restraining harness fits safely.

When you are making your choice, make sure that it has been tested and approved to the US government safety standards, and that it has a fastener that is easy for an unrehearsed adult to master in an emergency, yet not so easy that an inquisitive one-year-old can release it himself.

RESUMING NORMAL EXERCISE

If you have been following this exercise program conscientiously, by now not only will your body have recovered completely from the birth of your baby, but you may in fact be fitter than you were before pregnancy. Now you may want to think about maintaining that fitness through sports or other activities.

Making the right choice

Depending on how fit you were before your baby was born, and how regularly you have done your postnatal exercises, you may be able to introduce other sporting activities before the end of six months. Certainly swimming, walking distances, gentle yoga and cycling can be started by most women much earlier than activities such as jogging, or aerobic, fitness and dance classes. Games like tennis and racket ball, and especially squash, require absolute fitness before you start – they are not safe ways of attaining physical fitness. All exercise should be enjoyable and invigorating and should never be taken to the extremes of exhaustion or pain.

Basic advice

1 Don't exercise following a large meal or after drinking a lot of fluid.
2 Always warm up and slow down gradually before and after vigorous exercise; in cold weather muscles tend to contract and are more easily damaged, therefore make sure you are warmly dressed, especially for outside exercise.
3 Make sure that you have the right equipment for your sport – well-padded training shoes for running and loose, comfortable, absorbent clothing.
4 If you're taking up a new sport, such as running or aerobic classes, obtain really sound professional advice as to technique and local facilities. Beware of unqualified teachers and classes that are too large to be able to offer individual advice.
5 Don't push yourself beyond your own exercise tolerance; muscle "burning", overstretching and joint pain can be damaging and may result in your having to rest during a period of recovery.

Swimming

Swimming is an ideal way of getting fit safely. You can start as soon as you have stopped bleeding, though some women prefer to wait until after their postnatal check at six weeks. The water can provide both assistance (buoyancy removes the weight of gravity on the body) and resistance, so you can strengthen your muscles and mobilize your joints without the jarring stresses of land sports. If you are overweight, you are in fact more buoyant, and certain exercises can be easier for you (see page 109).

Swimming is wonderful exercise for the whole family and between three and six months, most babies happily take to the water in the security of their parents' hands

Simply swimming lengths of a pool is excellent exercise – the heart and lungs are working hard to take oxygenated blood to the muscles. The breaststroke is the most leisurely stroke, but it may aggravate backache; unless you keep your head well down in the water you may overarch your spine. The crawl or backstroke use more energy, and butterfly is only for the fit person. A relaxed way of swimming is on your back, using breaststroke movements of your legs, and supporting arm movements.

Specific exercises to be avoided

1 Lying on your back and lifting both straight legs together.
2 Sit ups from lying flat with legs straight. (Both numbers 1 and 2 involve risk of damage to back or abdominal muscles, and should only be done by athletes in training.)
3 Forced toe touching whether standing or sitting on the floor with legs straight. This can overstretch the spine and hamstring muscles if done in a bouncy, uncontrolled way.
4 'Bicycling' by balancing on your neck and shoulders, or rolling your legs back over your head so your toes touch the ground, can strain and damage the neck and upper back unless your body is well prepared.
5 'Bouncing squats' or 'squat thrusts' can damage the knee ligaments and cartilages. It is important to straighten your legs fully between squats.
6 Forcing your thighs apart by sudden pressure with your arms or hands overstretches your tendons and ligaments causing pain, and achieves nothing in terms of fitness. However, if you enjoy the sensation of a good stretch, make sure you allow your soft tissues to lengthen gradually.

Looking forward

Apart from the few warnings given above, exercise should always be fun. If you follow these few simple guidelines, you can safely enjoy any form of exercise – even pushing your carriage briskly to the shops. It will not only strengthen your muscles and improve your health, but will also give you a wonderful sense of achievement and well-being.

FURTHER READING

General

The Maternity Sourcebook : 230 Basic Decisions for Pregnancy, Birth, and Baby Care
Wendy and Matthew Lesko
Warner, 1984

Our Bodies, Ourselves
Boston Women's Health Book Collective
Simon and Schuster, 1976

Breastfeeding

Breastfeeding
Janice Presser and Gail Sforza Brewer
photographs by Julianna FreeHand
Knopf, 1983

The Breastfeeding Book
Máire Messenger
Van Nostrand Reinhold, 1982

Breast Is Best
Drs. Penny and Andrew Stanway
Academy Chicago, 1982

Childcare

Babyhood
Penelope Leach
Knopf, 1983

The Child Care Encyclopedia : A Parents' Guide to the Physical and Emotional Well-Being of Children from Birth through Adolescence
Penelope Leach
Knopf, 1983

Day-By-Day Babycare : An Owner's Manual for the First Three Years
Miriam Stoppard, M.D.
Villard, 1983

The First Three Years of Life
Dr. Burton L. White
Avon, 1978

Your Baby and Child : From Birth to Age Five
Penelope Leach
Knopf, 1978

Postnatal Depression

Depression after Childbirth : How to Recognize and Treat Postnatal Illness
Dr. Katharina Dalton
Oxford, 1980

Postnatal Depression
Vivienne Welburn
State Mutual, 1981

Relaxation and Exercise

The Baby Exercise Book : The First Fifteen Months
Dr. Janine Lévy
Pantheon, 1975

Simple Relaxation
Laura Mitchell
Atheneum, 1979

USEFUL ADDRESSES

American Foundation for Maternal and Child Health
30 Beekman Pl., New York, N.Y. 10022

American Public Health Association, Maternal-Child Health Section
1015 15th St. N.W., Washington, D.C. 20005

International Childbirth Education Association (ICEA)
5636 W. Burleigh St., Milwaukee, Wis. 53210

La Leche League International
9616 Minneapolis Ave., P.O. Box 1209, Franklin Park, Ill. 60131-8209

National Health Information Clearinghouse
P.O. Box 1133, Washington, D.C. 20013

National Home Safety Council, Home Safety Dept.
P.O. Box 11933, Chicago, Ill. 60611

National Women's Health Network
224 7th St. S.E., Washington, D.C. 20003

U.S. Consumer Product Safety Commission
Washington, D.C. 20207

INDEX

A

abdominal muscles
  anatomy of 17
  separation of 17
  and backache 17
afterpains 12
aggression 37
anxiety 35
areola 19, 66

B

baby
  bathing 121
  bouncers 121
  bouncing cradle 74, 95
  burping 66–8
  carriers 28, 64–6
  carrying 66
  car seat 123
  changing diaper 29
  colic 68–9
  cribs 69, 121
  development
    0 to 6 weeks 63–4
    6 weeks to 3 months 90–95
    3 to 6 months 113–19, 121
  development check 71
  strollers 28, 122
  swimming 121
  toys 64, 90, 121
  walkers 121
'baby blues' 34
backache 17, 24, 26, 29–31
  relieving 30–31
Back and Buttock Toner 57
back care 26–9
back muscles 19
Basic Pelvic Floor Exercise 52
bed
  getting out of 27
  reinforcing your 29
Bottom Walking 83
bowel movements, difficulty with
  15, 18
breasts 18–19
breastfeeding
  positions of comfort 42
  stimulation of involution 12
breathing for relaxation 41
  and exercise 48, 49
buggy, choosing 28, 122
Buttock Firmer and Back
  Strengthener 81
buttock muscles 19

C

Caesarean section 26
  exercises for 55–6
calories, extra for breastfeeding
  21
car seat, baby 122
carriage, choosing 28, 69
carrying baby, ways of 64–6
Cat Arch 30, 84
cervical erosion 16
circulation
  breathing for 49
  foot exercises 50
  hemorrhoids 52
clots, blood 14
changing diapers 29
coccyx 10
colic 68–9
colostrum 18
constipation 18
contraception 16, 71
coughing, and pelvic floor 16
cribs 69
crisis measures
  for exhaustion 35
  for tension 42
Curl-ups 54
Cycling 101

D

Daily program
  0 to 6 weeks 62
  6 weeks to 3 months 89
  3 to 6 months 112
depression 36–7
development see baby
diaper changing 29
diastasis recti 17, 18
diet 21
"Downcurler", the 82

E

edema 20
Elbow to Knee Twists 108
emotional changes 32
engorgement 18–19
episiotomy 14
equipment, baby
  0 to 6 weeks 63–9
  6 weeks to 3 months 95
  3 to 6 months 113–20
exercises
  first thoughts on 48

exercises cont'd
  general rules for
    123–4
  for mother
    first 48 hours 49–54
    0 to 6 weeks 49–62
    6 weeks to 3 months 74–89
    3 to 6 months 99–112
  for baby
    6 weeks to 3 months 90–94
    3 to 6 months 113–20
  breathing for 48
  resuming normal 124

F

face, relaxation of 41
fatigue 34
feeding, positions for 25, 42
Foot Exercises 50
Full Sit-ups 105

G

guilt, sense of 15

H

hemorrhoids 16, 26
heat, for perineal pain 15
Hip and Waist Trimmer 77
housework, positions 27–8

I

ice
  for perineal pain 15
  for hemorrhoids 16
incontinence, stress 16
intercourse
  pain during 15, 71
  positions for 15
intervertebral disc damage 30
involution of uterus 12, 71

J

jaws, relaxation of 41
joint changes 22

K

Knee Rolling 102
Kneeling Twists 106

L

Leanbacks 107
Leg Sliding 53
libido 37
lifting 28
ligaments, softening of 12, 22, 26
linea alba 17
lochia 12, 15
loneliness 36
lying on front 26

M

multiple births 18
muscles
 abdominal 17
 back 19
 buttock 19
 pectoral 18
 pelvic floor 14
 thigh 19

O

obesity 21
oblique abdominal muscles 17
older child, relationship with 35–6, 69

P

pain
 after 12
 from episiotomy or tear 14, 15, 24, 26
 on intercourse 15
parachute reaction 119
partner, relationship with 35
pectoral muscles 18
Pectoral Toner 60
pelvic floor 14–16
 exercises for 16, 55, 75, 99
 functions of 14
 structure of 14
 Ultimate Test for 99
Pelvic Floor and Stomach Trimmer 75
pelvic girdle, structure of 10
Pelvic Lift 100
pelvic organs 13
Pelvic Rocking 30, 60
perineum 14, 16

piles 16
play 90, 121
postnatal check-up 16, 71
postnatal depression 36–7
posture 22–6
 assessing 22
 correcting 24

Q

Quick Relaxation and Back Mobilizer 58

R

recti abdominis 17
relationships
 with older children 35–6
 with partner 35
relaxation 38–45
 breathing for 41
 comfortable positions 43
 crisis measures 42
 exercises for 44, 45, 58
 importance of 38
 post work-out 62, 89, 112
 technique for 40

S

sacroiliac joints 10
 maneuvers to relieve pain 30, 31
 pain 29
sacroiliac ligaments 26
sacrum 10
Scissors 103
separation of recti abdominal muscles 17, 18
sexual intercourse, positions for 15
sexual problems 15, 35
Side-bender 79
shoes 26
shoulders, relaxation for 40
sitting, correct 27
sleep
 catching up with 34
 crisis measure 35
slings, baby 28, 64–6
Squat Tightening 99
standing, correct 27
Stomach and Back Toner 86

Stomach Flattener and Waist Slimmer 78
stress 35
 crisis measures 42
 effects of 38–40
stress incontinence 16
stroller, choosing 28, 122
swelling, of legs 20
swimming 109–11, 123–4
 with baby 120, 122
symphysis pubis 10, 12

T

Tail-wagging 85
tension 38
test for
 stress incontinence 99
 separation of recti abdominis 52
Thigh and Hip Firmer 80
Thigh Firmer 87
thigh muscles 19–20
transverse abdominal muscles 17
toys 64, 90, 121

U

ultrasound, for perineal scar tissue 15
'Upcurler', the 76
Useful Resting Position and Buttock Toner 54
uterus 12
 involution of 12

V

vagina 16

W

Waist, Hip and Thigh Trimmer 104
Waist Swing 111
Waist Twister 61
 at swimming pool 109
Waist Whittler 59
Wall Press-ups 88
Water Curl-ups 110
weight loss 20

ACKNOWLEDGMENTS

Publisher's acknowledgments

The publishers would like to thank the following families for allowing themselves to be photographed for this book:
Julie, Paul and Adèle Cronin
Lucinda, Henry, Clare and Nicholas Zarb
Linda, Tom, Tania and Katie Davies
Joanna and Ruth Pambakian, Frances and Jesse Parker, and all the mothers at the Hammersmith Hospital postnatal exercise classes.
The Ajanta rug was kindly supplied by Habitat Designs Ltd.

Illustrations

Anatomical illustrations by Elaine Anderson
Figure illustrations by Howard Pemberton
Daily program figure illustrations by Russell Barnett

Editor Nicky Adamson
Art editor Caroline Hillier
Designer Anne Fisher
Series editor Pippa Rubinstein

Art director Debbie MacKinnon

ABOUT THE AUTHORS

Margie Polden has worked in obstetrics for 30 years as a qualified physiotherapist, running prenatal and postnatal classes in major London teaching hospitals and has co-written a small book and individually written many articles on her subject.

Barbara Whiteford has been qualified as a physiotherapist for 13 years. With specialist training in obstetrics and pediatrics, she teaches postnatal exercise classes and works with babies and their parents in hospitals and in their homes. She has two young children and lives in London.

Carolyn B. Coulam, M.D. is professor of obstetrics and gynecology at the Mayo Clinic in Rochester, Minnesota.

Authors' acknowledgments

The authors would like to thank the following:
Professor Murdoch Elder and all the midwives at the Hammersmith Hospital, London, for their advice and for allowing us to make use of the hospital facilities; Jill Hens (District Dietician at St Mary's Hospital, London, for her professional advice; Nicky Adamson, Pippa Rubinstein, Caroline Hillier and Sandra Lousada for their guidance, support and creativity; and especially our husbands, Iain and Martin.